MASTERS OF ART

THE ART OF
THE RENAISSANCE

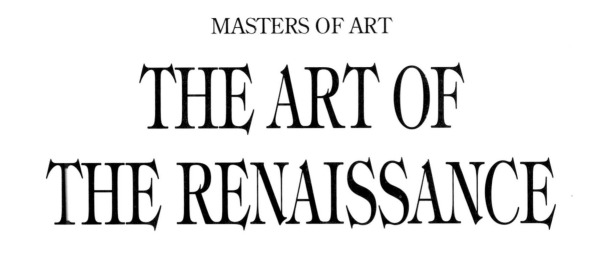

Lucia Corrain

◆

ILLUSTRATED BY
L. R. Galante, Simone Boni

PETER BEDRICK BOOKS
NEW YORK

DoGi

Produced by
DoGi, Florence
Original title:
L'Europa del Rinascimento
Text:
Lucia Corrain
Illustrations:
L.R. Galante
Simone Boni
Visualization:
Sergio
Picture research:
Katherine Forden
Graphic design:
Oliviero Ciriaci
Art direction and page design:
Sebastiano Ranchetti
Editing:
Andrea Bachini
Renzo Rossi
English translation:
Anthony Brierley
Editors, English-language edition:
Nathaniel Harris
Ruth Nason

© 1997 DoGi s.r.l.
Florence, Italy

English language text © 1997 by
DoGi s.r.l./Peter Bedrick Books

Published by
PETER BEDRICK BOOKS
2112 Broadway
New York, NY 10023
Library of Congress
Cataloging-in-Publication Data
Corrain, Lucia.
[Europa del Rinascimento. English]
The art of the Renaissance / Lucia
Corrain ; Illustrated by L. R. Galante,
Simone Boni. –1st ed.
p. cm. – (Masters of art)
Includes index.
Summary: An illustrated survey of
the art and culture of Renaissance
Europe.
ISBN 0-87226-526-9
1. Art, Renaissance – Juvenile litera-
ture. [1. Art, Renaissance. 2. Art
appreciation.] I. Galante, L. R., ill. II.
Boni, Simone, ill. III. Title. IV. Series:
Masters of art (Peter Bedrick Books0
N6370.C59513 1997
709'.02'4–dc21 97–19338
ISBN 0-87226-526-9

Cataloging-in-Publication Data is
available for this book by request
from the Library of Congress,
Washington, D.C., or from the
publisher.

Printed by Conti Tipocolor
Calenzano (Florence)

Photolitho
Venanzoni DTP, Florence
First edition 1997

◆ HOW THE INFORMATION IS PRESENTED

Every double-page spread is a chapter in its own right, devoted to a particular place that was important in the Renaissance period or to a type of art characteristic of the time. The theme of each spread is introduced in the main paragraph on the left (1) and in the large central illustration. Historical background information is given in the left-hand column. Other elements on the page, including reproductions of paintings and drawings, give more detailed insights into the main theme.

Some pages are devoted to major artists of the Renaissance period. Their works are considered and compared, in order to show the new ideas and techniques they introduced and developed.

The text in the columns at the sides of these double pages (1) provides a brief account of the artist's life, background information on the period or places concerned, or an analysis of art techniques.

CONTENTS

LEADING FIGURES

The period in European history known as the Renaissance spanned the 15th and 16th centuries and brought with it profound changes in all areas of life. Underlying these changes was a new awareness of what human beings could achieve; Renaissance scholars and thinkers, known as humanists, claimed that man was "the measure of all things". In art, the Renaissance started in Florence, Italy, during the early years of the 15th century. It reached its full expression in the 16th century in Italy, France, Germany, Spain, England, and the Netherlands. Architects, painters, and sculptors, inspired by the art and ideas of ancient Greece and Rome, had discovered a new way of representing form and space by applying the principles of perspective and the study of proportion. This book introduces the leading figures and key events of the Renaissance by taking the reader on a journey through the most important countries, cities, and courts of the time.

✦ **TURA AND MANTEGNA**
Two great northern Italian painters of the 15th century, among the first to adopt the innovations of Florentine artists such as Donatello.

✦ **GRÜNEWALD, CRANACH, AND DÜRER**
The three leading German Renaissance artists. Grünewald's intensely emotional work belongs to the late Gothic tradition. Cranach's art was refined and sometimes sinister in atmosphere. Dürer's art distinctively combined northern introspection with Italian humanist values.

✦ **EL GRECO**
Spanish painter of the 16th century, noted for the haunting spirituality of his works, and for his dramatic use of color.

✦ **FEDERICO AND LORENZO**
Masters of Urbino and Florence in the 15th century, these two were enlightened rulers of flourishing Renaissance courts.

✦ **MASACCIO AND PIERO DELLA FRANCESCA**
Two great pioneers of Renaissance painting, applying the new technique of perspective to create 3-dimensional effects.

✦ **VAN EYCK AND PIETER BRUEGEL**
Flemish painters of the 15th and 16th centuries whose art was notable for its realism and meticulous attention to detail.

✦ **QUEEN ISABELLA OF CASTILE**
Her support of Christopher Columbus at the end of the 15th century led to the discovery of the "new world" of America.

ISABELLA D'ESTE ✦
Under her patronage, great artists and scholars gathered at the court of Mantua, making it a brilliant center of Renaissance culture.

◆ FRANCIS I AND CHARLES V
The king of France and his rival, the Holy Roman Emperor. Their courts were centers of art and learning during the first half of the 16th century.

◆ FOUQUET AND COUSIN THE ELDER
Fouquet was a great French painter and miniaturist of the 15th century, his compatriot Cousin an eminent artist and designer of the 16th.

◆ TITIAN AND GIOVANNI BELLINI
Venetian Renaissance painting originated in the 15th century with Giovanni Bellini and culminated in the 16th century with Titian.

◆ RAPHAEL AND LEONARDO
Raphael's sense of harmony made him the exponent of pure beauty unsurpassed among Renaissance painters. Leonardo, who excelled in all the arts and sciences, is regarded as the great "universal" artist of the Renaissance.

PHILIP II ◆
King of Spain for over forty years (1556-98), and heir to a large part of Charles V's empire. Philip was a zealous champion of the Catholic Church and patron of the arts.

BRUNELLESCHI ◆ AND DONATELLO
Architect and sculptor. Inspired by classical art, they made 15th-century Florence the first great Renaissance center.

◆ HOLBEIN AND HENRY VIII
Holbein was a famous German court painter, strongly influenced by the Italian Renaissance. He worked for Henry VIII, the king of England (1509-47), who broke away from the Roman Catholic Church.

◆ MICHELANGELO AND JULIUS II
A vigorous, tormented artist, Michelangelo was employed by the warlike Pope Julius II (1503-13). Working for Julius in Rome, he created some of the greatest masterpieces of Renaissance art.

RENAISSANCE EUROPE

In the centuries after the fall of the Western Roman Empire in the 5th century A.D., Europe was relatively poor and backward. China, the Byzantine Empire, and the Abbasid Caliphate enjoyed a wealth, stability, and civilized way of life that were unknown in Europe. But from the 11th century, Europe experienced a period of growth and expansion, and by the 15th century even more profound developments were in train. Economic changes, new ideas, technological progress, and wars fought with large armies transformed European society. The medieval world of feudalism and chivalry gradually disappeared as small local authorities were replaced by large centralized states. Rulers freed themselves from traditional restraints, aiming for absolute power. Great European monarchs competed in lavish displays of wealth and taste, while relations between them were increasingly regulated by the art of diplomacy.

✦ **ARTISTS' TRAVELS**
During the Renaissance, artists were able to move about freely all over Western Europe. Exchanges between Spain and the Low Countries were favored by political links between the two countries. German artists made long journeys to work abroad or learn new skills. Italian artists were in even greater demand. All this led to the creation of a common artistic language that was universally understood.
The courts of kings and popes were the most sought-after destinations. Leonardo and Andrea del Sarto worked at the court of Francis I. Dürer stayed in Venice. Titian was invited to Augsburg by Charles V. Rulers used artists as their ambassadors, almost as if they were gifts that could be made to political allies.
The cultural and artistic innovations of the 15th century traveled quickly along well-trodden trade routes, and the spread of humanist ideas was further accelerated by the invention of printing. The new importance placed on education led to the foundation of universities everywhere.

Above:
Raphael, portrait of Leonardo, detail from *The School of Athens*, c.1510; Stanza della Segnatura, Vatican, Rome.

✦ **PARIS 1573**
In the gardens of the new Tuileries palace, Polish ambassadors offered the crown of Poland to Henri de Valois, brother of Charles IX, the king of France.

✦ **MUSICIANS**
Standing on an artificial rock, they are dressed in costumes inspired by Greek mythology. The statue at the top represents Apollo.

AMBASSADORS ✦
Representatives of the Venetian Republic and Russia meet with envoys of the Ottoman Empire at the French court.

HENRI DE VALOIS ✦
(1551-1589)
Henri was the younger brother of Charles IX, whom he succeeded in 1574, after only one year as king of Poland.

THE DELEGATION ✦
The visiting Polish party in traditional costume, perhaps feeling slightly awkward amid the refined elegance of the Parisian court.

CATHERINE ♦ DE MÉDICIS
(1519-1589)
Florentine by birth, she became the queen of Henri II of France. She helped to establish Italian Renaissance culture at the French court, which she dominated first as the queen regent and later as the queen mother.

CHARLES IX ♦
(1550-1574)
The second son of Catherine de Médicis. He came to the French throne at the age of ten and was dominated by his mother throughout his reign.

♦THE EUROPEAN SCENE
At the end of the 15th century there were 3 modern centralized states in Europe: France, Spain, and England. The Holy Roman Empire and Italy were still patchworks of smaller independent states.

♦ PAOLO UCCELLO
Battle of San Romano, 1456; tempera on panel, 182 x 317 cm. (6 ft. x 10 ft. 5 in.); National Gallery, London.

♦ HANS HOLBEIN THE YOUNGER
The Ambassadors, 1533; tempera on panel, 207 x 209 cm. (81.5 x 82.25 in.); National Gallery, London.

♦VITTORE CARPACCIO
Arrival of the Ambassadors of Britain at the Court of Brittany, 1495-96; tempera on panel, 275 x 589 cm. (9 ft. x 19 ft. 4 in.); Accademia, Venice.

THE REVIVAL OF ANTIQUITY

Italy became a center of trade and manufacturing in the 11th century, while most of Europe remained feudal. In the late Middle Ages, as France, Spain, and England developed into powerful centralized nations, Italy, though wealthy, remained a patchwork of middle-sized principalities and city-states. The early 15th century in Italy was marked by numerous political conflicts, but in 1454 the Peace of Lodi ushered in a period of relative calm, in which Renaissance culture approached its zenith. Noble courts and wealthy families patronized artists and scholars, and the influence of the Church, in particular of the papal court in Rome, stimulated the development of the arts. But the Renaissance also received much of its impetus from an ever-growing admiration for antiquity – above all for ancient Rome. The art, literature, and way of life of the ancient Romans provided Italians with models which they sought to equal if not surpass.

♦ RESCUING A WORK OF ART
During excavations at the foot of the Capitol in Rome, a Corinthian capital is being cleaned. It is what remains of the Temple of Concord, originally built in the 4th century B.C. and rebuilt by the Emperor Tiberius in the 1st century A.D. The capital is almost intact. Drawings will be made of it and measurements and proportions will be noted down.

♦ THE ITALIAN STATES
Italy in the 15th century was made up of five main states (the Duchy of Milan, the Republic of Venice, the Republic of Florence, the Papal States, and the Kingdom of Naples), plus small city-states like Urbino, Ferrara, and Mantua, and small republics like Siena and Lucca.

STUDY ♦ AND IMITATION
Rome, with its immense heritage of ancient ruins, was an irresistible attraction for artists from as early as the 15th century. Brunelleschi and Donatello went there from Florence in 1402.

The remains of a row of Ionic columns that may have formed part of a temple dedicated to Saturn.

BELVEDERE APOLLO ♦
2nd century A.D.; Vatican, Rome. Classical works of art discovered in Rome in the 15th and 16th centuries were a great inspiration to Renaissance artists. In designing their buildings, for example, architects used the proportions of the classically beautiful human body, which was regarded as the ultimate expression of perfection.

♦ **HUMANISM**
Humanism is a relatively modern term, used to describe the outlook of Renaissance thinkers, scholars, and writers. Such people are themselves known as humanists. They were steeped in the literature and philosophy of ancient Greece and Rome, which were "rediscovered" – or at least more thoroughly explored and understood – during the Renaissance. Humanists extolled what they believed to be the values of antiquity, notably a human-centered and this-worldly outlook, as opposed to the other-worldliness of the Middle Ages. Similar values influenced Renaissance artists, who delighted in human beauty, reintroduced the nude, and humanized previously remote religious figures and events. Some of the leading humanist thinkers in Italy were Coluccio Salutati (1331-1406), Giovanni Pico della Mirandola (1463-94), Lorenzo the Magnificent (1449-92), who founded a Platonic academy in Florence, and Marsilio Ficino (1433-99), who attempted to integrate classical philosophy with the Christian religion.
Above: portrait of Marsilio Ficino, detail from Domenico Ghirlandaio, *Angel Appearing to Zacharias*, 1490; fresco, 250 x 450 cm. (8 ft. 2 in. x 14 ft. 9 in.); Tornabuoni Chapel, Santa Maria Novella, Florence.

♦ **FROM TEMPLE TO CHURCH**
Columns of the Temple of Antoninus and Faustina, which was converted into a Christian church.

♦ **THE PAST RE-EMERGING**
The stones of ancient buildings and the surviving ruins of Roman monuments, like the huge vaults of the Basilica of Maxentius, were often incorporated into later structures.

FLORENCE

Florence was the cradle of the Renaissance, or "rebirth", of the arts. The idea of such a revival had gained ground in the city ever since Giotto had painted a series of masterpieces in the late 13th and early 14th century. But it was at the start of the 15th century that a revolutionary new style was created by a number of Florentine artists, including the architect and sculptor Filippo Brunelleschi. He conceived of architecture in a new way, and developed a system of perspective which he introduced into art. On his return from Rome in 1410, he found Florence at the height of its prosperity. Its guilds and merchants were financing great artistic and architectural projects, of which one of the most remarkable was the ambitious idea of crowning the cathedral with the largest dome built since antiquity.

♦ THE CITY
Founded in Roman times, Florence really began to prosper only from the 11th century. By the start of the 14th century the population had grown to 100,000, making the city one of the largest in Europe. At the beginning of the 15th century Florence was flourishing. Textile manufacturing, banking, and the gold florin of Florence, first minted in 1252, were the foundations of its prosperity. For long periods its economic and political life was controlled by powerful merchant guilds. Although Florence preserved its republican institutions, one family, the Medici, eventually came to dominate the city. Above: gold florin, with the lily, the city's emblem, on one side. On the other side was the city's patron saint, St. John the Baptist. Below: Jacopo Pontormo, *Cosimo the Elder,* posthumous portrait, c.1518 (detail); oil on panel, 86 x 65 cm. (34 x 25.5 in.); Uffizi, Florence. Cosimo was the first Medici ruler, holding all real power but leaving the old institutions intact.

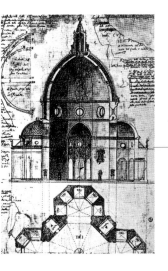

♦ THE DOME
Section of the dome of Florence Cathedral; drawing, c.1440. The double-shelled dome measures 43 m. (141 ft.) in diameter. It is slightly smaller than the dome of the Pantheon in Rome, which was the largest dome in the ancient world.

MARBLE ♦
From an ox-drawn cart workers unload a block of marble that has to be cut and prepared. Pulley blocks connected to a large three-speed winch are used to raise the stone and move it.

♦ FLORENCE CATHEDRAL
The building of the Cathedral in Florence was begun in 1296 by Arnolfo di Cambio (c.1232 - c.1302). It was continued by Giotto (1267-1337), who also designed the bell-tower. Work proceeded slowly throughout the 14th century and ended in 1436 with the closing of the void in the center of the dome.

MATERIALS ♦
A finished block of white marble that will be used for the rib in the high part of the dome.

♦ THE DOME
In 1433 work on the dome was at an advanced stage. It was being carried out at the level of the gallery above the large round windows of the drum, and on the two rows of small windows in the dome itself.

♦ VIEW
A view from above of Renaissance Florence.

♦ THE BUILDING SITE
A high fence marks the boundary of the building site. Dozens of laborers, stone-masons, carpenters, blacksmiths, and mechanics are at work, divided into teams under the leadership of a master-builder.

Filippo Brunelleschi, Pazzi Chapel, 1430; Church of Santa Croce, Florence.

♦ FILIPPO BRUNELLESCHI
(1377-1446)
The works of this great architect are distinguished by the lightness and harmony of the structures, by their classical proportions, and by his mastery of perspective and spatial effects. Brunelleschi designed the churches of San Lorenzo and Santo Spirito, the Foundling Hospital, the Pazzi Chapel, and the Pitti Palace.

Piero della Francesca, *Annunciation,* c.1470 (detail); oil and tempera on panel, 122 x 194 cm. (48 x 76.5 in.); Galleria Nazionale dell'Umbria, Perugia.

♦ PERSPECTIVE
Artists use perspective to achieve a realistic, three-dimensional representation of objects on a flat surface. The laws of perspective are based on lines that converge on a vanishing point. Objects are made to look smaller, the further away they are from the observer. Brunelleschi's perspective system was put into theoretical form by Leon Battista Alberti (1404-72).

ROPES ♦
Two laborers carry a heavy length of rope on their backs, sharing its weight between them.

Ropes were vital for transmitting the muscle power of humans or animals to machines to make them work.

FLORENTINE SCULPTURE

The story of Orsanmichele, a building in the center of Florence, helps us to understand what was happening at the beginning of the 15th century. Orsanmichele was an old grain market which had been converted into a church, with 14 niches in its outer walls. The municipal council ordered each city guild to place a statue of its patron saint in one of the niches. The works that were made were an impressive demonstration of the skill of contemporary sculptors such as Ghiberti, Nanni di Banco, and Donatello. At this time, Florentine architects and sculptors, unlike painters, worked mainly on public commissions. Generally speaking, there was less supervision by their patrons, and so sculptors were freer than painters to experiment. Consequently, sculpture was the first of the arts to be truly innovative, and succeeded in representing reality with the new language of the Renaissance.

♦ THE COMPETITION
In 1401 the guild of wealthy merchants in Florence, known as the Calimala, held a competition to decide who would be commissioned to execute the second bronze door of the Baptistery of Florence Cathedral. Competitors had to make a bronze panel portraying the Sacrifice of Isaac. After a rigorous preliminary selection two artists were left in the competition: Lorenzo Ghiberti and Filippo Brunelleschi. The entire city was divided between partisans of one or the other of the two artists. Ghiberti's harmonious style, with its naturalistic touches, was in complete contrast to Brunelleschi's innovative representation of space. In the end the committee of judges decided in favor of the elegance of Ghiberti's model.

Above and below: *Sacrifice of Isaac*, bronze reliefs for the Baptistery door, 1401, by Lorenzo Ghiberti (above) and Filippo Brunelleschi (below); Bargello Museum, Florence.

♦ ST. GEORGE
Donatello, *St. George*, 1415-16; marble, height 378 cm. (6 ft. 5 in.); Bargello Museum, Florence. The statue was commissioned by the Armorers' Guild of Florence. The figure of St. George stands firmly and realistically on the ground, very much in contrast to the older Gothic tradition of sculpture.

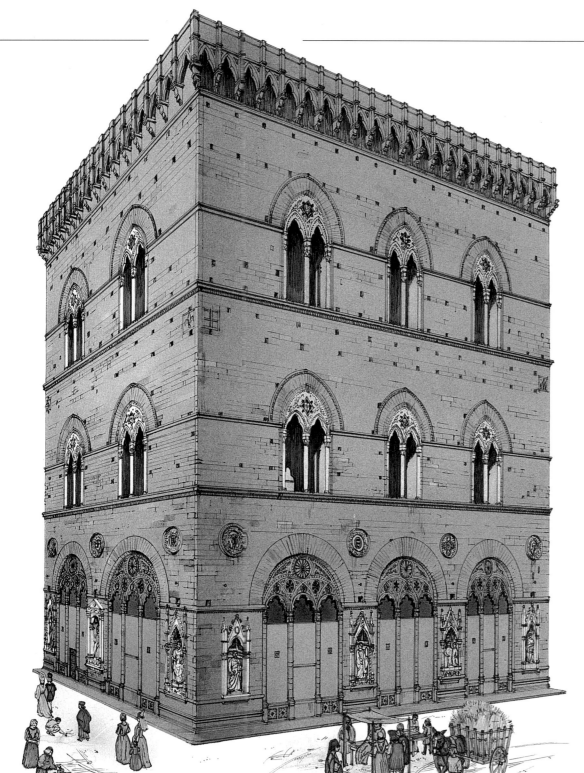

♦ St. John the Baptist
Lorenzo Ghiberti,
St. John the Baptist,
1412-16; bronze,
254 cm. (8 ft. 4 in.)
high; Orsanmichele,
Florence.

♦ Donatello
Donato di Niccolò
Betto Bardi, better
known as Donatello
(c.1386-1466), began
his artistic career as
one of Ghiberti's
assistants on the
north door of the
Florentine Baptistery.
From Brunelleschi he
learned the principles
of perspective, which
he brilliantly applied
to low-relief work.
He also mastered the
new relationship
between form and
space and adapted it
in his statues, which
he made in a range of
materials – marble,
bronze, terracotta,
wood. The vibrant
pictorial quality of
his sculpture was a
great inspiration
to the artists of
northern Italy, in
particular Mantegna
and Bellini.
Above:
Donatello,
Feast of Herod, 1427;
bronze relief for
baptismal font;
Baptistery, Siena.

♦ Orsanmichele
The sculpted figures
made for the niches
in the outside walls
of Orsanmichele
between 1410 and
1428 mark a turning-
point in the
history of art.

♦ Lorenzo Ghiberti
(1378-1455)
A typical Renaissance
artist, Ghiberti was a
sculptor, goldsmith,
architect, painter, and
art scholar. Between
1402 and 1424 he
made the north door
of the Florentine
Baptistery, and
between 1425 and
1452 the ten panels
of the east-facing
"Doors of Paradise".
Above:
Lorenzo Ghiberti,
St. Matthew, detail.

♦ Four Martyrs
Nanni di Banco,
*Four Crowned
Martyrs ("Quattro
Coronati")*,
c 1410-12; life-size
marble figures;
Orsanmichele,
Florence.

♦ St. Matthew
Lorenzo Ghiberti,
St. Matthew, 1419-22;
bronze, 270 cm.
(8 ft. 10 in.) high;
Orsanmichele,
Florence.

MASACCIO

♦ **MASACCIO**
Tommaso di ser Giovanni Cassai, better known as Masaccio, was born in 1401 in San Giovanni Valdarno, not far from Florence.
He showed a prodigious artistic talent at an early age and started his very brief working career in 1422.
In 1425, with Masolino da Panicale (1383-1440), he began a great fresco cycle in the church of the Carmine in Florence, commissioned by the wealthy Florentine merchant Felice Brancacci. The frescoes mainly narrate the life of St. Peter, the first bishop of Rome, shown in episodes of intense grandeur and drama.
Masaccio worked almost all his life in Florence, but died in Rome in 1428, at the age of 26 or 27.
His works include the *Madonna and Child with St. Anne and Angels,* executed with Masolino, and the Pisa Polyptych, later dispersed, which includes an *Enthroned Madonna and Child* and a *Crucifixion.*
More than fifty years later the frescoes of the Brancacci Chapel were completed by Filippino Lippi (1457-1504), the pupil of Botticelli.
Above: self-portrait of Masaccio. Detail from *The Raising of the Son of Theophilus,* 1427-28; fresco, 230 x 598 cm. (90.5 in. x 19 ft. 7.5 in.); Brancacci Chapel, Santa Maria del Carmine, Florence.

The representation of reality, mastered by Florentine sculptors of the Early Renaissance, soon found an equivalent in the paintings of another Florentine, the youthful Masaccio. In the famous fresco cycle in the Brancacci Chapel, Masaccio placed solid, lifelike human figures within what appeared to be real space. Noble and dignified, they interact convincingly with one another. In his last fresco, *The Trinity,* Masaccio made striking use of perspective technique, painting a chapel whose coffered barrel vault recedes behind the figures in the foreground so that the space represented actually looks like a niche carved into the wall of the church. Masaccio probably died at the early age of twenty-seven, but his pictorial innovations made him the founder of the main Renaissance tradition in painting.

♦ **THE TRINITY**
Masaccio, *The Trinity,* 1426-28; fresco, 640 x 317 cm. (21 ft. x 10 ft. 5 in.); Santa Maria Novella, Florence.
In this painting Masaccio employs perspective to create an illusion of depth, and charges the figures with an intense realism.
The Virgin Mary turns toward us full of sorrow.
St. John stands to the right of the cross, behind which God the Father appears as a majestic patriarch.

♦ **THE BRANCACCI CHAPEL FRESCOES**
The fresco cycle starts with *Adam and Eve tempted by the Serpent* and the subsequent *Expulsion,* 1425, reproduced left; 214 x 90 cm. (7 ft. x 2 ft. 11 in).
Three episodes are represented in *The Tribute Money,* 1425 (whole above and detail right); 247 x 597 cm. (8 ft. 1 in. x 19 ft. 7 in.). In the center of the painting Jesus tells Peter where to find the money; on the left of the picture Peter takes the money from a fish's mouth; and on the right Peter hands the money to the tax-gatherer at Capernaum.

✦ ST. PETER BAPTIZES THE NEOPHYTES

The Brancacci Chapel fresco cycle continues with *St. Peter Baptizing the Neophytes*, 1425 (whole left and detail right); 247 x 172 cm. (8 ft. 1 in. x 5 ft. 8 in.). Here Peter baptizes those who believe the word of Christ. The structure of the painting is simple and well-balanced. St. Peter and the kneeling man in the foreground are surrounded by a semi-circle of figures. standing in front of mountains that form the background.

✦ ST. PETER DISTRIBUTES ALMS TO THE POOR

The Distribution of the Goods and the Death of Ananias, 1426-27 (whole left and detail right); 232 x 157 cm. (7 ft. 7 in. x 5 ft. 2 in.). Here Peter is distributing alms to the poor. Ananias has been reproached for holding back part of his goods and is struck down. The other central figure, of a woman with a child receiving alms, shows great intensity of expression.

✦ ST. PETER HEALS A GROUP OF MEN

St. Peter Healing with His Shadow, 1426-27 (whole left and detail right); 232 x 162 cm. (7 ft. 7 in. x 5 ft. 4 in.). This story of St. Peter follows that of Ananias in the Acts of the Apostles. Peter walks along a street casting his healing shadow over a group of cripples. The sense of movement is enhanced by the effect of depth created by the buildings painted in perspective. Many believe that Masolino painted the man with the red cap.

THE SUPREMACY OF LINE

Masaccio's life was so short that he could hardly have become the leader of a "school" of painting. But his example had an enormous impact on Florentine art of the 15th century. Many later painters – Fra Angelico, Andrea del Castagno, Antonio del Pollaiuolo, Verrocchio, Filippo Lippi, Ghirlandaio, Botticelli, and Filippino Lippi – used Masaccio's innovations as the basis for experiments with light, color, perspective, and the harmonious arrangement of forms in space. Perhaps what these artists shared most, however, was a belief in the prime importance of line. The use of drawn outlines in painting was considered fundamental in giving a solid, sculptural quality to forms and creating a more exact representation of reality.

FIRST HALF OF ✦
THE 15TH CENTURY
1. Filippo Lippi, *Madonna and Child with the Birth of the Virgin*, 1452; panel, diameter 135 cm. (53 in.); Pitti Palace, Florence.
2. Andrea del Castagno, *Last Supper*, 1447; fresco, 470 x 975 cm. (15 ft. 5 in. x 32 ft.); Convent of Sant' Apollonia, Florence. Filippo Lippi sought to attain a refined beauty in his art. Andrea del Castagno aimed for intensity of expression.

✦ **GEOMETRIC ACCURACY**
Fra Angelico, *Annunciation*, c.1438; fresco, 230 x 321 cm. (7 ft. 1 in. x 10 ft. 6 in.); Monastery of San Marco, Florence. The illusion of depth is conveyed by a precise rendering of the receding columns and arches of the portico.

THE MASTERS ✦
1. Andrea del Verrocchio, *Head of St. Jerome*, c.1460 (detail); tempera on paper glued on panel, 49 x 46 cm. (19.5 x 18 in.); Pitti Palace, Florence.
2. Domenico Ghirlandaio, *Miracle of the French Notary's Child*, 1480; fresco; Sassetti Chapel, Santa Trinita, Florence. Leonardo da Vinci began painting in Verrocchio's workshop. The young Michelangelo was a pupil in the workshop of Ghirlandaio.

DEVOTION ✦
Fra Angelico, *St. Dominic at the Foot of the Cross*, 1442; fresco, 237 x 125 cm. (7 ft. 9 in. x 4 ft. 1 in.); Monastery of San Marco, Florence. Guido di Piero, better known as Fra Angelico (c.1400-55), worked as an artist in the service of the Dominican Order. This painting, in which the founder of the order prays by the cross, exemplifies Fra Angelico's religious devotion.

THE MEDICI CIRCLE ✦
1. Filippino Lippi, *Adoration of the Magi*, 1496; oil on panel, 258 x 243 cm. (8 ft. 5 in. x 8 ft.); Uffizi, Florence.
2. Sandro Botticelli, *Birth of Venus*, c.1483-85; tempera on canvas, 172 x 278 cm. (5 ft. 9 in. x 9 ft. 2 in.); Uffizi, Florence. Botticelli's art was perhaps the most sensitive expression of the outlook of the Medici court and of Florentine humanism in general. The *Birth of Venus* is an allegory in which love is seen as the driving force of nature. Botticelli's pupil, Filippino Lippi, developed a softer, essentially poetic style.

Antonio Pollaiuolo,
St. Sebastian, 1475;
tempera on panel,
292 x 203 cm.
(9 ft. 7 in. x 6 ft. 8 in.);
National Gallery,
London.

♦ **FLORENTINE
ARTISTS
OF THE 15TH
CENTURY**
The Florentine
artists of the Early
Renaissance were
directly influenced by
the revolutionary art
of Donatello and
Masaccio.
Filippo Lippi was
born in Florence
in 1406 and died in
Spoleto in 1469.
He was the father of
Filippino Lippi.
Andrea del Castagno
was born in about
1423 in the Tuscan
Apennine village of
Castagno; he died in
Florence in 1457,
having also worked in
Venice and Rome.
Andrea del
Verrocchio was born
in Florence in 1435
and died in Venice in
1488. He was a
goldsmith, sculptor,
and painter. By the
1470s his workshop
was one of the most
famous in the city,
rivaling that of
Antonio Pollaiuolo.
Pollaiuolo was born
in Florence in 1431
and died in Rome
in 1498.
Domenico
Ghirlandaio was born
in Florence in 1449
and died in 1494. He
was the greatest
pictorial chronicler
of his age.
Sandro Botticelli,
the creator of an
exquisite and
mysterious art, was
born in 1445 in
Florence, where he
died in 1510.

Domenico Veneziano, detail of St. John.

♦ THE ST. LUCY ALTARPIECE

Time and accident have scattered many works of art that originally belonged together. This is the case with the St. Lucy altarpiece (1445-47), whose six parts are now housed in four different museums.

The altarpiece represents the "holy conversation" between Mary and four saints. The predella (beneath the main scene) contains the Annunciation and the miracles of the saints.

1. *Madonna and Child with St. Francis, St. John the Baptist, St. Zenobius, and St. Lucy,* tempera on panel, 209 x 216 cm. (82 x 84 in.); Uffizi, Florence.
2. *St. Francis Receives the Stigmata,* tempera on panel, 26.7 x 30.5 cm. (10.5 x 12 in.); National Gallery of Art, Washington, DC (Kress Collection).
3. *St. John the Baptist in the Desert,* tempera on panel, 28.3 x 32.4 cm. (11.1 x 12.75 in.); National Gallery of Art, Washington, DC (Kress Collection).
4. *Annunciation,* tempera on panel, 27.3 x 54 cm. (10.75 x 21.25 in.); Fitzwilliam Museum, Cambridge, England.
5. *Miracle of St. Zenobius,* tempera on panel, 28.6 x 32.5 cm. (11.25 x 12.75 in.); Fitzwilliam Museum, Cambridge, England.
6. *Martyrdom of St. Lucy,* tempera on panel, 25 x 28.5 cm. (9.8 x 11.25 in.); Gemäldegalerie, Berlin.

THE PAINTING OF LIGHT

In the 1440s a new painting style appeared in Florence, based on the use of gradations of color as a means of representing light. Its leading exponent was Domenico Veneziano ("the Venetian"), whose painting of the St. Lucy altarpiece provides the best illustration of the technique. The altarpiece also reveals the advances made in the use of perspective to produce an illusion of depth, and shows the importance of Domenico's influence on one of the giants of 15th-century Renaissance art, his sometime pupil Piero della Francesca.

♦ **ANNUNCIATION**
Domenico Veneziano, *Annunciation.*
The skilled use of perspective gives depth to the graceful colonnaded court leading through into a flowered garden. The crystalline light reflected by the architecture has the same quality as that in the altarpiece.

Piero della Francesca,
Baptism of Christ,
detail.

♦ **PIERO DELLA
FRANCESCA**
Piero della Francesca
was born in Borgo
Sansepolcro, near
Arezzo, between
1410 and 1420.
Around 1435, in
Florence, he became
an apprentice in the
workshop of
Domenico Veneziano,
with whom he
executed frescoes for
the choir of
Sant'Egidio.
In 1445 he began the
*Misericordia
Polyptych* of Borgo
Sansepolcro, which
he finished in 1462.
One of his most
celebrated
achievements was
the famous cycle of
frescoes on the
*Legend of the True
Cross* for the church
of San Francesco in
Arezzo, which he
completed in 1459.
He worked in Rome,
Urbino, Ferrara, and
Arezzo, but was
indifferent to worldly
success and spent
most of his life in his
native town, where he
died in 1492.
His absence from the
great Italian courts
accounts for the
modest appraisal he
received after his
death, although in
some places his
influence was
considerable.
Today, many art
historians regard
him as the greatest
Italian painter of
the 15th century,
the founder of an
artistic style that
was the perfect
synthesis of linear
perspective
and light.

♦**SUBLIME COLOR**
Piero della Francesca**,**
Baptism of Christ,
1448-54; tempera on
panel, 167 x 116 cm.
(66 x 45.75 in.);
National Gallery,
London.
Christ's face, though
rugged, is also serious
and sensitive. The
skin has the same
pictorial quality as
the shaggy beard
and hair, a sublime
example of the
luminosity that can be
achieved with color.

♦**SCULPTED FIGURES**
Piero della Francesca,
*Madonna and Child
with Saints,* 1472-74;
oil on panel, 248 x
170 cm. (98 x 79 in.);
Brera, Milan.
The grouping and
rich draperies remind
us of the regular
arrangement in
Domenico
Veneziano's
paintings. Here the
figures have a more
sculptural quality
than those in the
Baptism of Christ.

♦**PERSPECTIVE**
Paolo Uccello, *Miracle
of the Host,* 1465-69
(details); tempera on
panel, 43 x 351 cm.
(16.5 in. x 11 ft. 6 in.);
Galleria Nazionale delle
Marche, Palazzo
Ducale, Urbino.
According to legend,
Paolo Uccello was
obsessed with the new
science of perspective.
The scene on the left is
relatively conventional,
with the vanishing
point in the center of
the wall. In the other
scene the vanishing
point is to the right of
the outer wall. This
puts a strain on
Alberti's system of
perspective; the effect is
not wholly convincing.

URBINO

The sudden rise and equally rapid decline of Urbino is closely bound up with the career of its duke, Federico da Montefeltro. A brave condottiere (mercenary soldier) and man of culture, Federico was the very personification of a Renaissance lord. His palace, the work of Luciano Laurana, was considered the finest of its time and was so big that it was almost impossible to distinguish its buildings from those of the small town surrounding it. Scientists and illustrious architects worked at the court of Urbino, and the figurative arts were distinguished by experiments in perspective and proportion. The most important artist to work in Urbino was Piero della Francesca. Both the Sienese architect Francesco di Giorgio Martini and Leon Battista Alberti also worked at the court, and the High Renaissance architect Donato Bramante spent his formative years in the city.

♦ THE PALACE CITY
The ducal palace, which took thirty years to build, was described as the Palace City. The various parts of the complex were carefully built into the existing town, thus respecting its layout which originated in ancient Roman times. The palace and the town are perfectly integrated, a successful expression of the urban ideal.

♦ THE TOWN
Urbino is in central Italy. From the 14th century the Montefeltro family became increasingly important, and under Federico, lord of Urbino from 1444, this quiet little hill town became the home of one of the most brilliant courts in Italy. Federico da Montefeltro (1422-82) had received his education in Mantua, at the court of the Gonzaga family, and was a celebrated condottiere (mercenary soldier) who had fought in the armies of Venice, Naples, Florence, and the Papacy. It was in fact Pope Sixtus IV who conferred on him the title of duke in 1474. During a tournament he lost his right eye, which is why he is always shown in left profile. A cultured man, he had a library of over 1100 books on science and the arts of war.
Above and below: Piero della Francesca, portraits of Federico da Montefeltro and his wife Battista Sforza, *Montefeltro Diptych*, 1465; oil on panel, both 47 x 33 cm. (18.5 x 13 in.); Uffizi, Florence.

♦ PIERO DELLA FRANCESCA
Flagellation, c.1460 (whole left and detail below left); oil and tempera on panel, 59 x 81.5 cm. (23.25 x 32.1 in.); Galleria Nazionale delle Marche, Palazzo Ducale, Urbino. This work shows Piero's mastery of perspective. But the enigmatic subject of the painting has puzzled art scholars, who have interpreted its meaning in different ways. The main area of uncertainty concerns the identity of the three characters in the foreground, to the right of the flagellation. What connection is there between the two groups? And why is the flagellation taking place in the background? Some scholars claim that the young man dressed in red is Oddantonio da Montefeltro, the half-brother of Federico, who was killed in a conspiracy in 1444. If this is true, then the figures to his left and right are possibly the assassins, Manfredo del Pio and Tommaso d'Agnello.

FORMAL GARDENS ♦
The duchess's quarters overlooked the gardens, which contained a large greenhouse.

THE COURTYARD ♦
This courtyard is surrounded by Laurana's delightful arcade. The left wing contains the splendid throne room, the largest in the palace.

THE CORTILE ♦ DEL PASQUINO
Looking onto this courtyard were the quarters reserved for ambassadors and diplomats. The mezzanine floors were occupied by servants' rooms.

♦ CITY OF DREAMS
Ideal City, late 15th century; tempera on panel, 67.5 x 239 cm. (26.5 in. x 7 ft. 10 in.); Galleria Nazionale delle Marche, Urbino. A circular-plan building in the classical style stands in a large square. The painting is by an unknown central Italian artist.

♦ IDEAL CITIES
Architectural plans devised in the first half of the 15th century were based on symmetry, regularity, and exact calculation. The plans were made for individual buildings, and not for cities, which underwent no significant overall changes in this period.

The abrupt fall in the population from the middle of the 14th century, caused by the Black Death, meant that local authorities lacked the time and money needed to support large-scale building schemes of the kind undertaken during the Middle Ages.

Spurred by Renaissance ideals, artists and architects planned ideal cities, but these were never built. The only exception was the town of Pienza in central Italy, built entirely by Pope Pius II, Enea Silvio Piccolomini (1405-64).

Above and below: The Cathedral and the Town Hall, Pienza.

♦ THE CORTILE DEL GALLO
Overlooking this courtyard were quarters reserved for illustrious guests.

♦ THE KEEP
By means of a spiral ramp wide enough for horses to pass through, the keep linked the palace with the "Piazza d'Armi", used for markets and parades. The adjacent low wing was a stable for over 300 horses.

THE GATEHOUSE ♦
The mighty gatehouse, with its towers and internal stairways, housed Federico's quarters overlooking the valley.

FERRARA

The rulers of Ferrara, the Este, adopted a sumptuous lifestyle that was characteristic of Italian Renaissance courts, attaching great importance to displays of courtly ritual and chivalry. It was a custom to stage lavish festivities for the benefit of illustrious guests, and nowhere were these more popular than at the court of the Este dukes, who claimed descent from King Arthur's knights of the Round Table. In the 15th century, when the city was dominated by buildings that symbolized its rulers – the Castle and the Este Palace – an artistic school developed there whose leading exponents were Cosimo Tura, Francesco del Cossa, and Ercole de' Roberti. The art of the Ferrarese painters, inspired by Piero della Francesca and Donatello, was full of its own distinctive imagination and enchantment. It demonstrated the way in which Renaissance culture assumed an independent character in places outside the main artistic centers.

♦ THE CITY
Ferrara was situated between the more powerful cities of Milan and Venice, but under the Este lords it developed into one of the most flourishing and influential centers of Renaissance culture. In the 15th century the city was ruled by Niccolò III (1393-1441), and later by his three sons: Lionello (1441-1450), Borso (1450-1471), and Ercole (1471-1505). Duke Borso put on lavish spectacles and spent huge sums on palace decorations, a richly illuminated Bible, and the rebuilding of the Este summer palace, the Palazzo Schifanoia. In Ferrara, as elsewhere, painters were paid by the square meter, at a rate that varied according to the ability and reputation of the artist and the quality of materials used. Some materials could be very expensive. All the well-paid work of Cosimo Tura (c.1430-93) in the Sala dei Mesi cost less than illuminating the Bible referred to above. Above and below: Cosimo Tura, *Madonna Enthroned with Musician Angels*, c.1480 (details); oil on panel, 239 x 101 cm. (94 x 39.75 in.); National Gallery, London.

CHURCHMEN ♦
The presence of prelates and a papal legate lends solemnity to the official ceremony. Later, the whole court will assemble in the cathedral for mass.

THE PALACE ♦
The ducal apartments in the Este palace have been completely redecorated for the occasion. They must be worthy of a future queen.

AMBASSADORS ♦
The representatives of foreign rulers take part in the festivities, wearing the brightly colored costumes of their native lands.

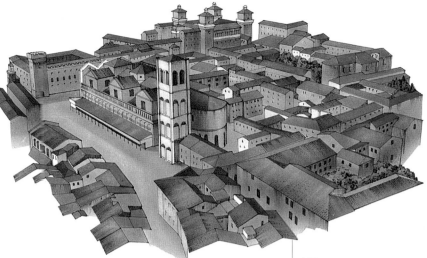

♦ **VIEW**
A view of Ferrara, the city ruled by the Este family.

THE CASTLE ♦
The castle of San Michele stands next to the Este palace, to which it is linked for security reasons.

The defense towers and the wide moat surrounding the castle make it a formidable stronghold.

♦ **THE JOUST**
Horsemen prepare to take part in a joust on the parade-ground.

♦ **COSIMO TURA**
Spring, c.1460; oil on panel, 116.2 x 101 cm. (45.75 x 39.75 in.); National Gallery, London.

♦ **COSIMO TURA**
Madonna Enthroned with Musician Angels, c.1480; oil on panel, 239 x 101 cm; National Gallery, London.

♦ **OFFICIAL WELCOME**
Under the ceremonial canopy, Duke Ercole d'Este and his wife Eleonora welcome Beatrice and her retinue of Neapolitan dignitaries.

Leon Battista Alberti, design for Sant'Andrea, Mantua, 1472.

Mantua

Andrea Mantegna painted in a powerful sculpturesque style and was a virtuoso in the use of perspective. He was fortunate in the place of his birth, Padua, a city near Venice which employed such Florentine masters as Donatello, Filippo Lippi, and Paolo Uccello, whose innovations were then absorbed by the Venetians. Recognized as one of the great masters of his age, Mantegna established the longest and most continuous of working relationships between an artist and a Renaissance court. For 46 years, from 1460 until his death in 1506, he was the official painter of the Gonzaga family, lords of Mantua. During this time his work ranged from the production of theater machinery and tapestries to portraits and decorations for the palaces and villas of Lodovico III. As marquis of Mantua, Lodovico drove forward the great urban renewal of the city, to which a decisive contribution was made by the architect Leon Battista Alberti.

♦ **ARCHITECTS**
A major feature of Mantua's great architectural and urban renewal was the church of Sant'Andrea, the work of Leon Battista Alberti (1404-72). Its gigantic barrel-vaulted interior was copied all over Europe, and for its façade Alberti used the motif of coupled pilasters rising the entire height of the building. Alberti evidently found Lodovico Gonzaga's court in Mantua a stimulating environment and, besides the church of Sant'Andrea, he also built the church of San Sebastiano in the city. During his Mantuan period Alberti employed his repertoire of ancient models with ever-increasing freedom. Later, Raphael's pupil Giulio Romano (1499-1546) followed Alberti in the use of giant pilasters in the Palazzo del Tè in Mantua. Below: Giulio Romano, detail of a façade of the Palazzo del Tè, 1525-26, Mantua.

♦ **THE DUCAL PALACE**
The history of the Ducal Palace in Mantua was closely bound up with the Gonzaga family, who held court in this grand and extravagant residence between 1328 and 1707. Isabella d'Este (1474-1529), the cultivated wife of Francesco Gonzaga, played an important role in making Mantua a great center of Renaissance culture.

♦ **FALCONRY**
The art of breeding and training falcons, sparrowhawks, goshawks, and kites enjoyed great popularity among the nobility in the Renaissance period.

♦ **SEIZE THE PREY!**
The lord holds the hooded falcon on his left fist. Beside him rides the falconer, who has trained the bird to hunt. With an upward swing of the arm and a sharp shouted command the lord launches the bird. The hunting party follows the falcon's swooping flight, guided also by the sound of a bell attached to one of its talons.

THE CAMERA PICTA ✦ (PAINTED CHAMBER)

Mantegna's frescoes depict episodes from the life of the Gonzaga family. On the north wall is the family group with courtiers and messengers (right). Possibly this scene shows Lodovico being handed a letter from Bianca Maria Visconti announcing the illness of her husband, Francesco Sforza, duke of Milan, and summoning Gonzaga, his military commander. The fresco on the west wall shows grooms and horses at the ready, and Lodovico meeting his sons Federico and Francesco.

✦ DETAILS

Frescoes on the walls of the Camera Picta (Painted Chamber), 1465-74; Ducal Palace, Mantua. Lodovico Gonzaga (left) is recognizable in the scene showing the Gonzaga family and court (above).

Andrea Mantegna, ceiling oculus; fresco, diameter 270 cm. (8 ft. 10.25 in.); Camera Picta, Ducal Palace, Mantua.

✦ MANTEGNA

Andrea Mantegna (1431-1506) was the first artist in northern Italy to absorb thoroughly the artistic innovations of Masaccio and Donatello. Mantegna was born in Isola di Carturo, near Padua. He started his artistic apprenticeship in the Paduan workshop of Francesco Squarcione, whose passion for classical antiquities deeply influenced his pupil. In 1453 Mantegna married Nicolosia, the daughter of the famous Venetian painter Jacopo Bellini. He worked in Padua, in the Ovetari Chapel, and in Verona, where he painted the San Zeno altarpiece (1456-59). On August 7, 1460, he entered the court of the Gonzagas in Mantua and, except for brief visits to Florence and Rome, spent the rest of his life in their service. In 1474 he completed the frescoes of the Camera Picta. Among his other masterpieces are the *St. Sebastian* in the Louvre and the *Dead Christ* in the Brera, Milan.

✦ THE HUNT

In the countryside just outside Mantua a falcon hunt is in progress. Falcons, like horses, were regarded as creatures of great nobility. Hunting parties were made up of the lord and his courtiers, often accompanied by ladies.

✦ THE PACK

Greyhounds, basset hounds, bloodhounds, and spaniels seek out and retrieve the prey. Their trainers reward them with pieces of raw meat.

MILAN

In the 1490s Milan enjoyed a period of economic prosperity and a cultural flowering. The court of Lodovico, known as "il Moro", was one of the most splendid in Europe, and he himself one of the most enlightened Renaissance rulers. Hoping to make his city the Athens of Italy, he invited humanists, painters, and architects to his court. Among the projects on which the architect Bramante worked was the monastery of Santa Maria delle Grazie, where Leonardo painted his famous *Last Supper* on the wall of the refectory. Lodovico had scientific as well as artistic leanings, and the presence of engineers and mathematicians at the court encouraged Leonardo in his own research and observations of nature. At the end of the century foreign invasions led to the fall of Lodovico il Moro, the end of the Sforza dynasty, and the city's decline.

Bonifacio Bembo, *Portrait of Francesco Sforza*, 1460; tempera on canvas, 49 x 31 cm. (19.25 x 12.25 in.); Brera, Milan.

♦ THE VISCONTI AND THE SFORZA
In the 15th century Milan was the most powerful state in Italy. Its ruler, Gian Galeazzo Visconti (1385-1402), had advanced eastward toward Venice and expanded his possessions in central Italy. When he died, power passed to his son Gian Galeazzo Maria (1402-12), then to his other son Filippo Maria (1412-47), the last of the Visconti. The succession was won by the condottiere Francesco Sforza (1450-66), who was succeeded by the young Galeazzo Maria. Galeazzo was murdered in 1476, leaving a seven-year-old son. In 1479 this boy passed under the control of his uncle Lodovico il Moro. On his nephew's death in 1494 Lodovico made himself duke.
In 1499 the Sforza dynasty was overthrown by Louis XII of France and the duchy of Milan fell under foreign control.
Below: Bonifacio Bembo, *Portrait of Bianca Maria Sforza*, 1460; tempera on canvas, 49 x 31 cm. (19.25 x 12.25 in.); Brera, Milan.

♦ SANTA MARIA DELLE GRAZIE
Originally a small oratory containing a miraculous image of the Madonna of the Rosary. In 1463 the monastic complex was added. From 1497 it housed the chapter of the Lombard congregation of the Dominican Order.

♦ THE LAST SUPPER
Leonardo da Vinci, *The Last Supper*, 1495-97; tempera on wall, 460 x 880 cm. (13 ft. 9 in. x 29 ft. 10 in.); Refectory, Santa Maria delle Grazie, Milan.
The painting treats a traditional subject – Jesus announcing his impending betrayal – in a new way. It is stripped of any superfluous content, so that it expresses the astonishment and utter dismay of the disciples.

THE PRIOR ♦
Vincenzo Bandello, adviser to Lodovico il Moro, has obtained permission to modify the original layout of Santa Maria delle Grazie and enlarge the entire complex.

THE THREE ARTISTS ♦
Bramante and Amadeo were the architects who worked on the building of Santa Maria delle Grazie. Here they are in discussion with Leonardo da Vinci.

♦ THE LANTERN AND THE TRIBUNE

The lantern, a sixteen-sided gallery with thirty-two two-arched bays, is the work of Giovanni Antonio Amadeo (1447-1522). Below it is the square tribune built by Donato Bramante (1444-1514).

Cameo with portrait of Lodovico il Moro; Museo degli Argenti, Florence.

♦ THE CLOISTER

Used as a burial ground for the monks. The east side housed the dormitory on two floors and the chapter. The north side housed a huge library of valuable manuscripts.

♦ LEONARDO IN MILAN

Sent to Lodovico il Moro by Lorenzo the Magnificent, Leonardo arrived in Milan in 1482. Here favorable circumstances enabled him to realize his artistic and scientific ambitions. It is probable that Leonardo and Bramante influenced each other, or rather that Leonardo's schemes for central-plan buildings played a significant role in the design of Santa Maria delle Grazie. This style of architecture was relatively new. The central plan became the means for integrating building elements into a single unit.

Florence 1504

The 16th century was the greatest age of Italian art and a high point in the history of western civilization. The first 30 years or so of the century are known as the High Renaissance. As early as 1504, the giants of High Renaissance art – Leonardo, Michelangelo, and Raphael – were all working in Florence. As a style term, "High Renaissance" describes the harmonious relationship achieved between the imitation of nature and artistic composition, between realism and idealization, and perhaps also between science and religion. The heyday of the High Renaissance in Florence was short-lived. In 1506 Leonardo returned to Milan. Michelangelo was called to Rome, where Raphael also began work in 1508. As a result, the papal court in Rome replaced Florence as the art capital of the Renaissance.

♦ MONA LISA
Leonardo da Vinci, *Mona Lisa*, 1503-14; oil on panel, 77 x 53 cm. (30.25 x 21 in.); Louvre, Paris. With this painting, which embodies his search for a perfect marriage between realism and harmony, Leonardo set a new standard for the art of portraiture.

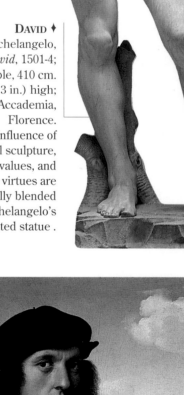

DAVID ♦
Michelangelo, *David*, 1501-4; marble, 410 cm. (14 ft. 3 in.) high; Accademia, Florence. The influence of classical sculpture, moral values, and civic virtues are masterfully blended in Michelangelo's celebrated statue .

♦ PALAZZO VECCHIO
The Palazzo Vecchio was the seat of government of the Florentine state. It was built from 1299, following the design of Arnolfo da Cambio, but in the course of time modifications were made. For example, an enormous room was added to the back of the medieval building, to accommodate the five hundred elected representatives of the people.

♦ THE "ROOM OF THE FIVE HUNDRED"
To decorate the walls of the great room, the Republic asked Leonardo and Michelangelo to paint two victorious episodes in the history of the Florentine state. Leonardo was asked to paint the *Battle of Anghiari*, Michelangelo the *Battle of Cascina*. Neither of the works has survived.

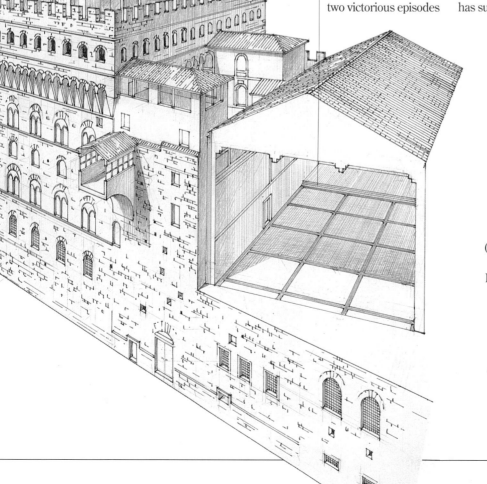

ANGELO DONI ♦
Raphael, *Portrait of Angelo Doni*, c.1506; oil on panel, 63 x 45 cm. (24.5 x 17.25 in.); Pitti Palace, Florence. Inspired by Leonardo and Michelangelo, Raphael created an art of sublime harmony and classical beauty, excelling as a painter of religious, mythological, and portrait subjects.

♦ **LEONARDO**
During the years he worked in Florence Leonardo re-created the art of portraiture. The naturalness and harmony of the celebrated *Mona Lisa* (details left and right) served as a model for generations of later artists.

♦ **MICHELANGELO**
When Michelangelo returned to Florence in 1501 he was already an established master. Fired by his enthusiasm for republican ideals, he set about transforming an enormous block of marble into the *David* (details left and right) – a symbol of political liberty.

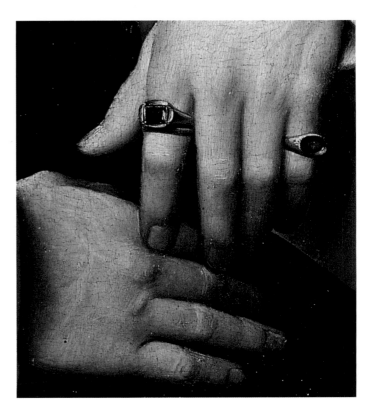

♦ **RAPHAEL**
During his four years in Florence (1504-8), Raphael executed a number of portraits for the families of the city's merchant aristocracy. Among them was a painting of the wealthy art patron Angelo Doni (details left and right). Inspired by Leonardo, Raphael portrays his sitter confidently dominating the space of the painting.

ROME

Julius II was elected pope in 1503. His papacy was notable for vigorous political and military campaigns to consolidate the Church's dominions, and for an unprecedented flourishing of the arts that made Rome the unrivaled center of High Renaissance culture. Building projects begun in the previous century under Popes Nicholas V and Sixtus IV were continued under the direction of Bramante, who designed the new church of St. Peter's. Michelangelo and Raphael were summoned to carry out important commissions in the Vatican, and in the Belvedere courtyard Julius assembled ancient statues and antiquities unearthed during excavations. In 1513 Julius II was succeeded by Leo X de' Medici (1513-21), under whose papacy Rome reached the height of its splendor.

Statue of the Emperor Claudius, first half of the 1st century A.D.; marble; Vatican, Rome.

♦ **THE PAPACY AT THE BEGINNING OF THE 16TH CENTURY**
At this time the Spanish had taken control of Naples and the French had occupied Milan. Between these foreign powers lay the States of the Church, and so the papacy played a pivotal role in Italian politics. Julius II (1503-13) led armies against the Venetians and the French. His successors were Leo X (1513-21) and, after the short-lived papacy of Adrian VI, Clement VII (1523-34). Clement's support for France proved disastrous for Rome, which was sacked by the imperial armies of Charles V in 1527. Clement VII was succeeded by Paul III, who ruled from 1534 to 1549. Below: Raphael, *Portrait of Leo X* (detail), 1516-19; tempera on panel, 154 x 119 cm. (60.5 x 47 in.); Uffizi, Florence .

♦ **LAOCOÖN**
Marble statue of the 1st century A.D., discovered on the Esquiline Hill in Rome in 1506. Cortile del Belvedere, Vatican, Rome.

♦ **SISTINE CHAPEL**
Michelangelo painted the ceiling of the Sistine Chapel for Julius II between 1508 and 1512.

♦ **ROME**
Engraving showing a view of Rome after the building of Sixtus V in 1602.

THE NILE ♦
This Hellenistic statue was unearthed in 1513 and purchased by Pope Leo X. Cortile del Belvedere, Vatican, Rome.

SANTA MARIA ♦
SOPRA MINERVA
The church contains frescoes by Filippino Lippi, Michelangelo's celebrated statue of the *Risen Christ*, and the tomb of Fra Angelico.

✦GALATEA
Raphael, *Galatea*,
1511; fresco,
295 x 225 cm.
(9 ft. 8 in. x 7 ft. 5 in.);
Villa Farnesina,
Rome.

**✦PALAZZO DELLA
CANCELLERIA**
This colossal palace
is so impressive that
it was traditionally,
but wrongly,
attributed to
Bramante.

**SAN PIETRO ✦
IN MONTORIO**
This small temple,
inspired by classical
models, was built by
Bramante from 1503.
Generally known as
the Tempietto, it is a
symbol of the
Renaissance.

VENUS FELIX ✦
Unearthed in
a garden of the
Campo dei Fiori, the
Venus Felix was
purchased in 1509 by
Pope Julius II.
Cortile Ottagono,
Vatican, Rome.

✦ VILLA MEDICI
This Renaissance
villa was built on top
of an earlier
construction in 1544.
The façade is bare
and austere, but the
loggia overlooking
the garden is well-
proportioned and
gracefully decorated.

PALAZZO FARNESE ✦
The palace was
begun in 1517 by
Antonio da Sangallo
the Younger, for
Cardinal Alessandro
Farnese, the future
Pope Paul III. It was
completed by
Michelangelo.

Michelangelo,
Libyan Sibyl, 1511;
fresco, 395 x 380 cm.
(12 ft. 11 in. x 12 ft. 6 in.);
Sistine Chapel,
Vatican, Rome.

♦ MICHELANGELO IN ROME

Michelangelo was
born in Caprese, near
Arezzo, in 1475 and
died in Rome in 1564.
As a young man he
lived and worked in
the Florence of
Lorenzo the
Magnificent, but most
of his later life was
spent in Rome. He
visited the city for the
first time in 1496 and
in 1498 carved the
celebrated *Pietà* there.
In 1505 Pope Julius II
summoned
Michelangelo from
Florence to Rome, to
create a monumental
tomb (this work was
never completed).
Between 1508 and
1512 Michelangelo
worked on the ceiling
of the Sistine Chapel,
and in 1536, after
another stay in
Florence, he began
the great fresco of the
Last Judgement. In
1547, by now the most
famous artist of his
time, he was appointed
architect of St. Peter's.
Below: Michelangelo,
Delphic Sibyl, 1511;
fresco, 395 x 380 cm.
(12 ft. 11 in. x 12 ft. 6 in.);
Sistine Chapel,
Vatican, Rome.

MICHELANGELO'S PROPHETS

In the years when he worked in Rome, Michelangelo
showed a particular interest in the Old Testament
prophets. The prophets were inspired by God, carrying
his messages to humankind and interpreting the events
of their time as expressions of divine providence. As the
main subject of Julius II's tomb Michelangelo chose the
awe-inspiring figure of Moses, whom the Jewish and
Christian traditions recognized as the greatest of all
prophets. On the ceiling of the Sistine Chapel he painted
another seven Old Testament prophets, remarkable for
their expressive power. In these works Michelangelo
went beyond the harmony and balance of the High
Renaissance, creating mighty figures of rugged
grandeur and great spiritual intensity.

♦ JONAH

The Book of Jonah
describes its hero as
an unwilling prophet.
When God summons
him to go to Nineveh
and denounce the
people's sins, Jonah
takes flight. Only
after being swallowed
by a great sea
creature does he
obey God and
successfully bring
the people to
repentance.
By Michelangelo's
day, Christians
interpreted Jonah's
deliverance from the
sea as a symbol of
the Resurrection.

♦ MOSES

Michelangelo,
Moses, 1515; marble,
235 cm. (7 ft. 8.5 in.)
high; San Pietro in
Vincoli, Rome.
A huge, never-
finished project, the
Tomb of Julius II,
tormented
Michelangelo for
years. The statue of
Moses was the most
important element of
the tomb completed
by Michelangelo
himself. The
awesome power of its
mighty form and its
noble gaze exemplify
the Renaissance
exaltation of man.
Moses was the great
liberator of the Jews
from Egyptian
slavery, guiding his
people toward the
promised land.

♦ **EZEKIEL**
One of the four "Greater" Old Testament prophets, perhaps active during the Babylonian exile. (c. 590 B.C.). His fantastic visions sometimes anticipate those in the Apocalypse.

JEREMIAH ♦
Like Ezekiel, one of the four major Old Testament prophets. Jeremiah was active from 626 to 587 B.C. During the Babylonian exile his was a voice of sorrow, but also of hope.

♦ **ISAIAH**
Active in the second half of the 8th century B.C., Isaiah was the greatest Old Testament prophet, expressing profound ideas through powerful images.

DANIEL ♦
The last of the four major prophets of the Old Testament, Daniel is said to have survived the lion's den and other terrors. The Book of Daniel was written in the 2nd century B.C., during the persecution initiated by the Syrian King Antiochus IV.

♦ **ZECHARIAH**
Zechariah was active just after the return of the Jews from exile in Babylon. The Book of Zechariah is the penultimate of the twelve Minor Prophets of the Old Testament.

JOEL ♦
One of the earliest Old Testament prophets (9th century B.C.?). After a plague of locusts had laid waste the land, Joel predicted an imminent Day of the Lord and called for repentance.

RAPHAEL AND THE VATICAN STANZE

Raphael,
Self-portrait, 1506; oil
on panel, 43 x 53 cm.
(17 x 20.75 in.);
Uffizi, Florence.

♦ LIFE AND WORKS
Raphael was born
in Urbino in 1483,
the son and pupil
of the painter
Giovanni Santi.
He continued his
artistic training
in the workshop
of Perugino in
Perugia, learning
from him how to
achieve naturalness
and harmony in the
representation of
human figures.
In Urbino he saw the
paintings of Piero
della Francesca and
successfully
assimilated the
artist's mastery
of space.
After a stay in
Florence, where he
met Leonardo and
Michelangelo,
Raphael was invited
to Rome by
Bramante, who
wanted the young
artist as his assistant.
Sensationally
successful, Raphael
worked in the
city from 1508 until
his death in 1520.
In 1517 he succeeded
Bramante as chief
architect of St Peter's.
Below: Raphael,
*Madonna of the
Goldfinch*, 1507;
oil on panel, 107 x
77 cm. (42 x 30 in.);
Uffizi, Florence.

One of the great artistic projects commissioned by
Pope Julius II was the decoration of four rooms, the
Stanze, in the Vatican. Raphael was summoned to
Rome in 1508 and replaced the artists who had been
working on the project: his master Perugino, Sodoma,
Bramantino, and Lorenzo Lotto. The young artist
completed the frescoes of the first two rooms, leaving
the other two to his assistants, notably Giulio Romano.
In the last two years of his brief life Raphael was in fact
preoccupied with the building of St. Peter's. In the
frescoes of the Vatican Stanze he demonstrated his
supreme mastery of harmonious composition and
color, and his ideal of humanity, in which he sought to
combine faith and intellect and goodness and beauty.

♦ HERACLITUS
Detail from *The
School of Athens*
(left). The isolated
figure of Heraclitus,
a Greek philosopher
of the 6th century
B.C., is in fact
Michelangelo, to
whom Raphael is
paying tribute.

♦ PHILOSOPHY
Raphael, *The School
of Athens*, c.1510;
fresco, base 770 cm.
(27 ft.); Stanza della
Segnatura,
Vatican, Rome.
The theme of this
painting, which faces
the one on theology
(below), is the
triumph of intellectual
or rational truth.

♦ THEOLOGY
Raphael, *Disputation
over the Sacrament*,
c.1509; fresco, base
770 cm. (27 ft.);
Stanza della
Segnatura, Vatican,
Rome.
The fresco is
concerned with
the doctrine of
the Eucharist and
represents the
triumph of
theological truth.
In Heaven, God the
Father, Christ, and
the Virgin are
enthroned among
saints. In the lower
register the doctors
of the Church are
debating the nature
of the sacrament.

♦ PLATO AND ARISTOTLE
Raphael put these two Greek philosophers of idealism and realism in the center of his composition. The face of Plato is a portrait of Leonardo. Detail from *The School of Athens*.

♦ DIOGENES
This curmugeonly Greek Cynic philosopher lived in the 5th-4th century B.C. Raphael pictures him sprawled across the steps in front of Plato and Aristotle. Detail from *The School of Athens*.

♦ PYTHAGORAS
The Greek philosopher and mathematician Pythagoras, who lived in the 6th century B.C., is shown at work, with book, pen, and inkwell. Detail from *The School of Athens*.

♦ THE VICAR OF CHRIST
Raphael, *Liberation of St. Peter from Prison*, 1513; fresco, base 660 cm. (21 ft. 8 in.); Stanza d'Eliodoro, Vatican, Rome. Raphael's frescoes in the second of the Stanze represent attacks on Christ's representative on earth, the pope. St. Peter was the first pope. The fresco cycle symbolizes the invincibility of the papacy, but there is also an implicit glorification of Julius II.

VENICE

The Renaissance was the golden age of Venetian art. In the later 15th century, while the republic struggled with political dangers following the fall of Constantinople, its artists created some of the most famous works in history, many of them now housed in museums all over the world. It is often said that Florentine painting was based on drawing, whereas Venetian art was distinguished by a virtuoso use of color. Of course, great Venetian painters such as Bellini, Carpaccio, and Titian were also excellent draftsmen. And yet there is no doubt that the importance of line, in Florentine painting, is matched by the direct use of color to create forms, in the work of the Venetians. Venice was a great center on the trade routes between Europe and the East, and new colors and high-quality pigments were widely available there. But it was the way in which color was used – with much variety of tones and a mastery of light effects – that characterized Venetian painting.

Giovanni Bellini, *Portrait of Doge Loredan*, c.1501; oil on panel, 62 x 45 cm. (24.5 x 17.75 in.); National Gallery, London.

♦ **THE CITY**
Venice was founded in the 6th century, when people from the mainland, fleeing from invaders, took refuge on a cluster of islets and mud flats in a shallow lagoon at the head of the Adriatic Sea.
The early settlers, who lived by fishing, formed a league of villages and elected a leader, the Doge.
In the 8th century the Doge established his residence in the center of the lagoon. Expanding trade and industry brought wealth and power, and by the end of the 13th century Venice had become one of the most powerful city-states in Europe.
During the 15th and 16th centuries Venice was involved in wars with the Ottoman Turks, who took Constantinople in 1453.
In 1571, the Venetians, in alliance with the Holy League, sank the Turkish fleet at the battle of Lepanto. Economic decline set in soon afterwards, however, and in 1797 Napoleon ended the city's independence. And yet, even in decline, Venice seemed able to generate amazing creative activity in art, literature, and music.

♦ **THE WEDDING**
Every year on Ascension Day Venice celebrated its "marriage" with the sea. The Doge embarked on the Bucentaur and threw a golden ring into the waters of the lagoon at San Nicolò di Lido, saying: "We marry you, O Sea, as a sign of our true and everlasting dominion."

THE BUCENTAUR ♦
30 m. (98 ft.) long and 8 m. (26 ft.) wide, this was the ceremonial barge of the Venetian Republic. It had two decks and was lavishly decorated and equipped with banners and canopies.

♦**THE PROCESSION**
With all the bells in the city ringing, a throng of boats of all kinds accompanies the Bucentaur's majestic outing to the Lido.

♦ THE LAGOON
The Grand Canal,
Venice's principal
waterway, follows
a serpentine course
through the heart
of the city.

♦ THE CHARACTER OF
VENETIAN ART
Renaissance Venice
was one of the
wonders of the world.
Its uniqueness as an
urban center rising
from the water was
matched by the
unique character of
its painting.
Venetian art was
shaped by a variety
of outside influences.
The Byzantine
tradition played a
significant role for
centuries, and the
influence of Islamic
culture was also
strong. In the 15th
century, as a result
of the ongoing
commercial and
diplomatic relations
between Venice and
the rest of Europe,
particularly Flanders
and Germany, the
city became a center
for the import of
Flemish paintings.
The visit to the city of
Antonello da Messina
in 1475-76 was of
great importance
(see page 39).
Above: Antonello da
Messina, *Self-portrait*,
1473; oil on panel,
35.5 x 25.5 cm.
(14 x 10 in.); National
Gallery, London.
Below: Antonello
da Messina,
Annunciation, 1475;
oil on panel, 45 x 34.5
cm. (18 x 13.5 in);
Galleria Nazionale,
Palermo.

♦ JUSTICE
In front of the upper
deck is a statue of
Justice. The figure
is holding the
traditional symbol
of a pair of scales.

♦ THE OARS
Twenty-three oars
on each side, each
operated by three
oarsmen in the lower
deck, move in perfect
unison – like two
huge wings.

GIOVANNI BELLINI

Giovanni Bellini was the great master of 15th-century Venetian painting. He came from a family of artists – both his father Jacopo and his younger brother Gentile were painters – at a time when Venetian painting was still dominated by a Gothic courtly style. The visits to Venice of Florentine painters, the art of his brother-in-law Andrea Mantegna, his contact with Flemish painting, and particularly the influence of Antonello da Messina, combined to transform Bellini's painting into a feast of color and light. His figures express intense emotion, while extraordinarily realistic landscapes are laid out behind them, suggesting a harmonious relationship between humanity and its environment.

Giovanni Bellini, *Greek Madonna*, c.1475; tempera on panel, 84 x 62 cm. (33 x 24.5 in.); Brera, Milan.

♦ **BELLINI'S LIFE AND ARTISTIC DEVELOPMENT**
Giovanni Bellini was the son of the Venetian painter Jacopo Bellini. He is thought to have been born in about 1432. The young Giovanni was trained in his father's workshop and was certainly influenced by the painting of his brother-in-law, Andrea Mantegna, from whom he learned how to give the human figure structure and solidity. More independently, he developed a strong feeling for color, for nature, and for the representation of human emotions. The landscapes he painted are clearly based on the rural areas of the Venetian mainland. Between 1470 and 1473, while painting an altarpiece in Pesaro, Bellini visited the court of Urbino, where he was able to see the paintings of Piero della Francesca. From these he learned how to render space by means of perspective and color. During the final years of his long life, he was appointed official painter to the Venetian Republic and continued to execute a large number of commissions. He died in 1516.

♦ **POLYPTYCH**
Giovanni Bellini, *Polyptych of St. Vincent Ferrer*. Top: Angel of the Annunciation, Dead Christ Supported by Angels, Virgin Mary; panels, each 72 x 67 cm. (28.5 x 26.5 in.). Middle: St. Christopher, St. Vincent Ferrer, St. Sebastian, panels, each 36 x 60 cm. (14.25 x 23.5 in.). Bottom: five episodes from the life of Vincent Ferrer, three panels, each 36 x 60 cm. (14.25 x 23.5 in.). Before 1464, Church of SS. Giovanni e Paolo, Venice.

♦ **THE DEAD CHRIST**
Giovanni Bellini, *Dead Christ Supported by Mary and St. John the Evangelist (Pietà)*, c.1467 (whole above and detail left); tempera on panel, 86 x 107 cm. (34 x 42 in.); Brera, Milan.

AN EARLIER EXAMPLE ♦
Giovanni Bellini, *Dead Christ Supported by Two Angels (Pietà)*, c.1452; panel, 74 x 50 cm. (29 x 19.75 in.); Correr Museum, Venice.

ST MARK'S SQUARE ✦
Gentile Bellini,
*Procession of the Relic
of the True Cross*,
1496; oil on canvas,
367 x 745 cm.
(10 ft. 7 in. x 14 ft.);
Accademia, Venice.

LANDSCAPE ✦
Giovanni Bellini,
Madonna and Child,
1508; oil on panel,
85 x 115 cm.
(33.5 x 45.5 in.);
Brera, Milan.

Giovanni Bellini,
San Giobbe altarpiece,
c.1478; panel, 471 x
258 cm. (15 ft. 5 in. x 8
ft. 5 in.); Accademia,
Venice.

✦**THE MEETING
WITH ANTONELLO
DA MESSINA**
Antonello da Messina
(1430-1479) was a
master of
atmospheric effects
and realistic detail in
the Flemish manner.
He was also a painter
of unsurpassed ability
in portraiture.
In 1475 he arrived in
Venice, where
Giovanni Bellini and
others learned from
his command of oil-
painting techniques,
in particular the
technique of creating
light effects. Bellini's
liberated color is
increasingly apparent
in the 1470s
and 1480s.
The *San* Giobbe
altarpiece exemplifies
the artistic debt of
Bellini and the
Venetians to
Antonello.
Below:
the figure of
St. Sebastian
from the San Giobbe
altarpiece.

INTENSITY ✦
OF EXPRESSION
Antonello da
Messina,
Condottiere, 1475; oil
on panel, 35 x 28 cm.
(13.75 x 11 in.);
Louvre, Paris.

✦**PORTRAIT**
Giovanni Bellini,
Portrait of a Man,
1480-90; panel,
32.8 x 25.5 cm.
(13 x 10 in.);
Louvre, Paris.

GIORGIONE

Giovanni Bellini ran a busy, successful workshop in Venice, from which emerged Giorgione and Titian, the two great innovators among 16th-century Venetian artists. Giorgione went even further than Bellini in creating convincing landscapes that envelop the human figures, making them part of an overall mood. He also increasingly dispensed with "drawn" outlines, using color to differentiate between objects; tonal changes, less abrupt than outlines, were more effective in integrating figures and background. Unfortunately, Giorgione died young, leaving only a handful of paintings that are indisputably his work.

Giorgione,
Enthroned Madonna and Child,
1504-5; panel,
200 x 152 cm.
(78.75 x 60 in.);
San Liberale,
Castelfranco Veneto.

♦ **GIORGIONE'S LIFE**
The life of Giorgione is something of a mystery. Born in Castelfranco Veneto in about 1478, he is believed to have served his artistic apprenticeship in the workshop of Giovanni Bellini. In about 1504 he painted an innovative altarpiece for San Liberale, Castelfranco. The figures were not enclosed in an architectural framework, as they had always been in the past, but were arranged in the shape of a pyramid with a wide landscape in the background. In 1508 Giorgione painted *The Three Philosophers*, remarkable for the intense expression of the human figures. He died, probably of plague, in 1510.
Below:
detail from
The Three Philosophers,
1508; oil on canvas,
123.5 x 144.5 cm.
(48.5 x 57 in.);
Kunsthistorisches
Museum, Vienna.

♦ **THE TEMPEST**
Giorgione, *The Tempest*, c.1508 (whole left and details above and below); oil on canvas, 82 x 73 cm. (30.25 x 28.75 in.); Accademia, Venice. Much of this small canvas is taken up by the storm. Giorgione has not placed his figures in a setting that merely serves as their background. Here nature dominates. Trees, light, air, clouds, the bridge, and the human figures are all parts of a unified whole.

♦ **CELEBRATION OF LIFE**
The precise meaning of Giorgione's painting *The Tempest,* and the identity of the figures in it, have been the object of considerable debate among art scholars.
Some interpret the scene as entirely a fruit of the artist's imagination, and consequently the first painting without a specific subject. Others see it as a portrayal of the artist's family. Some find its source in Ovid's *Metamorphoses*; others speak of personifications like Fortitude (the man) and Charity (the woman), living with Fortune (bolt of lightning). It has also been interpreted as a lost Eden. In 1569 the painting was called *Mercury and Isis*, the contemporary interpretation being that it represented the nymph Io suckling her child beside Mercury. Essentially, the subject of the painting is nature, a celebration of life's most fundamental forces.

TITIAN

Patronized by great European rulers, Titian dominated the 16th-century flowering of Venetian culture. The Renaissance in Venice was as momentous in its way as the earlier movement in 15th-century Florence and the spectacular, short-lived High Renaissance in Rome. As well as Bellini, Giorgione, and Titian, Venice numbered Veronese, Tintoretto, Paris Bordone, and Dosso Dossi among its master-painters; but the supremacy of Titian has never been disputed. He renewed religious art, brought portraiture to the heights of classical perfection, and created dynamic new versions of the allegories and mythological stories so dear to the Renaissance courts.

Titian,
Self-portrait,
1565-70; oil on canvas,
86 x 65 cm.
(34 x 25.5 in.);
Prado, Madrid.

✦ **TITIAN'S LIFE AND WORKS**
Titian was born in Pieve di Cadore in about 1490.
After working as an apprentice to Gentile and Giovanni Bellini, he came into contact with Giorgione, from whom he learned the new technique based on the dominant role of color in the rendering of form.
His own style was distinguished by the immediacy of the subjects he painted and the extreme naturalness of his human figures.
After the deaths of Giorgione in 1510 and Giovanni Bellini in 1516, Titian became the leading figure in Venetian painting.
In addition to private commissions, he now received many public charges.
In 1516 he painted an altarpiece with *The Assumption of the Virgin* for the Church of Santa Maria Gloriosa dei Frari.
In 1545, after working for the lords of Ferrara and Urbino, he was triumphantly received in Rome by Pope Paul III.
From 1550 he worked for Charles V and his son Philip II of Spain, to whom he sent the votive painting of the Battle of Lepanto, *Religion Saved by Spain*, in 1575.
He died in Venice in 1576, while plague was raging in the city.

✦ **THE MYTH**
Titian, *Danaë*,
1553-54; oil on canvas,
128 x 178 cm.
(50.25 x 70 in.);
Prado, Madrid.

✦ **THE EMPEROR**
Titian, *Charles V on Horseback*, 1548; oil on canvas, 332 x 279 cm.
(10 ft. 10 in. x 9 ft. 2 in.);
Prado, Madrid.

✦ **THE POPE**
Titian, *Pope Paul III with Alessandro and Ottavio Farnese*, 1546; oil on canvas, 210 x 174 cm. (6 ft. 10 in. x 5 ft. 8 in.); Capodimonte Gallery, Naples.

✦ **THE ALTARPIECE**
Titian, *Assumption of the Virgin*, 1516-18; oil on panel, 690 x 360 cm. (22 ft. 6 in. x 11 ft. 10 in.); Church of Santa Maria Gloriosa dei Frari, Venice.
With this *Assumption* Titian revolutionized altarpiece painting, injecting it with new emotional energy.

Titian's skill imbues Mary's Assumption with a sense of soaring movement, reinforced by the gestures of the crowd below. His use of color, based on a subtle interaction of warm browns, ochers, and reds, plays a crucial role in binding the various parts into a unified whole.

THE LOW COUNTRIES

Early in the 15th century, at about the same time as the Renaissance was beginning in Florence, painting entered a new and splendid phase in Flanders. In fact, it could be said that the most vigorous elements in 15th-century European art were Italian and Flemish painting. The two flourishing centers, Italy and Flanders, had one thing in common: the dominant influence of the merchant classes in political and economic life. There were also strong links between them. Italian merchant houses – mostly Genoese and Tuscan – had branches in large cities like Bruges, Ghent, Tournai, and Brussels, where the Italian banks were also operating. Some merchants became art connoisseurs, and their wealth enabled them to commission new work. Both Italian and Flemish painters benefited from the cultural interchange between the regions; and not only ideas but artists and works of art traveled from one to the other.

Rabbit-Hunting with a Ferret, c.1560 (detail); tapestry, 300 x 360 cm. (9 ft. 10 in. x 11 ft. 10 in.); M. H. D. Young Memorial Museum, San Francisco.

✦ THE INHERITANCE OF THE HABSBURGS

In 1384 the Duke of Burgundy took control of the Low Countries, with the exception of some large cities including Bruges, Ghent, Lille, Tournai, and Douai, which in the 12th century had declared themselves free communes.

In the 14th-15th century Burgundy became a European power, with one of the wealthiest and most splendid courts in Europe. In addition to the Low Countries, it controlled an area roughly equivalent to central France. The last Burgundian ruler, Mary, the daughter of Charles the Bold, married the Habsburg Maximilian I of Austria.

When Mary died in 1489 her territorial possessions, including the Low Countries, passed to the Habsburgs. They were later inherited by Maximilian's young grandson Charles I of Spain (1500-1558), who in 1519 became the Holy Roman Emperor Charles V.

Charles's son, Philip II, became king of Spain in 1556, and also inherited the Low Countries, which he subjected to heavy taxes and religious persecutions.

✦ THE LOW COUNTRIES
The Low Countries, an area corresponding to modern Benelux, consisted of 17 provinces. Flanders was one of the most important of these, because of its industrial development, and its name is often used to denote the entire southern Low Countries.

✦ TAPESTRY-WEAVING
Tapestries are hand-woven wall-hangings. A tapestry is sometimes also called an "arras", after the city of Arras which was a weaving center from the 13th century. The making of tapestries was one of the most important industries in the southern Low Countries from the 15th to the 17th century.

HORIZONTAL LOOM ✦
The yarns of the warp are stretched on the loom. The heddles, which lift the threads, are operated by pedals. The design, or cartoon, is placed under the warp so that the loomworkers can follow it as they weave.

♦ **TAPESTRY-WEAVING**
Tapestry-weaving is
regarded as an art
form, as it requires
technical skill and
sensitivity in the
choice of colors and
materials (wool, silk,
linen, as well as gold
and silver). The
designs, or cartoons,
were often created by
famous painters.

♦ **DYEING**
The yarns are
immersed in vats
containing alum
(which acts as a
mordant, or fixing
agent) and dye
powders: saffron for
the yellows, galls for
the blacks, and
Brazilian wood
for the crimsons.

THE COMMISSION ♦
The client agrees on
a price and delivery
date with the
workshop master,
while members of his
retinue admire a nearly
finished tapestry.

♦ **APPRENTICES**
Before being
promoted to work on
the loom, apprentices
had to learn all the
stages involved in
making a tapestry.
Apprenticeships were
long and regulated by
strict rules.

VERTICAL LOOM ♦
The threads of the
warp are stretched
between two rollers
operated by levers.

The tapestry-weaver
works on the back of
the tapestry, using a
mirror in front to
check his progress.

Hubert
and Jan van Eyck,
*The Adoration of the
Lamb* (detail).

♦ **FLEMISH PAINTERS
IN EUROPE**
Art historians have
identified three
fundamental qualities
in Flemish painting of
the 15th century:
a meticulous realism,
a brilliant rendering
of light, and multiple
symbolic meanings,
concealed in
everyday objects.
The influence of
Flemish painting in
Italy, particularly in
the south, was related
not to its symbolism,
but to its realism and
its treatment of light.
The impact of
Flemish painting was
also felt outside Italy,
in Provence, in the
Rhine Valley, and
in Spain.
The Italian artist
who most fully
assimilated the
meticulously detailed
realism of the
Flemish masters
was Antonello da
Messina. However,
Flemish influence is
also apparent in the
attention given to
landscape by other
artists, such as
Domenico Veneziano,
Piero della Francesca,
and Giovanni Bellini.
Italian merchants who
had lived in Flanders,
and the patronage of
the Italian courts,
were responsible for
the influx into Italy of
works by Jan van
Eyck (d.1441), Rogier
van der Weyden
(c.1400-1464),
Petrus Christus
(d.1473),
Hugo van der Goes
(d.1482), and
Hans Memling
(c.1435-1494).

15TH-CENTURY
FLEMISH PAINTING

A major feature of Flemish painting was the treatment
of space in both landscapes and interiors. The light-
flooded space in Jan van Eyck's paintings creates a
striking airiness and sense of depth. With his work,
painting began to engage with the real world. Italian
painters, and Florentine painters in particular,
approached the external world through perspective,
the study of the human body, and the application of
concepts of classical proportion. Flemish painters,
on the other hand, tackled it by meticulous attention
to details, which were assembled to provide a mirror
of the visible world. Behind their realistic surfaces,
Flemish paintings often contained a complex
symbolism: each object in the picture was included for
its own sake, but also stood for some momentous idea.

♦ **ROBERT CAMPIN**
*Virgin and Child
Before a Firescreen*,
1420-25; tempera on
panel, 63 x 49 cm.
(25 x 19 in.); National
Gallery, London.
Campin was the first
Flemish painter to
give a precise, jewel-
like rendering of
objects.
The use of a window
to picture a landscape
and add depth to an
interior was a great
innovation.

♦ **THE VAN EYCKS**
*The Adoration of the
Lamb,* 1420-32 (whole
above and detail left);
oil on panel, 137.7 x
242.3 cm. (54.2 x
95.4 in.); Cathedral
of St. Bavon, Ghent.
This work was begun
by Hubert van Eyck
in about 1420 and
finished by his brother
Jan in 1432. It consists
of twelve panels, of
which eight – the
wings – are painted
on both sides.
In the upper part, from
left to right: Adam,
rejoicing angels, the

Virgin Mary, God the
Father, St. John the
Baptist, musician
angels, and Eve.
In the lower part:
the righteous judges,
the knights of Christ,
the Adoration,
hermits, and pilgrims.
The detail shows the
altar with the bleeding
Lamb, the symbol of
Christ's sacrifice.
Pilgrims converge
from the four corners
of the earth. The
complex composition
is unified by the light
of an enchanted
landscape.

◆AN ITALIAN MERCHANT
Jan van Eyck, *Giovanni Arnolfini and his Wife*, 1434; oil on panel, 82 x 60 cm. (32.25 x 23.6 in.); National Gallery, London.
One of the great achievements in the history of painting. As well as being intensely realistic, the work is full of symbols. The mirror represents purity, but is also the instrument by which the presence of a witness is revealed; the dog is a symbol of fidelity.

Jan van Eyck, *Portrait of Margaret van Eyck*, 1439 (detail); oil on panel, 41.2 x 34.6 cm. (16.2 x 13.6 in.); Groeningemuseum, Bruges.

◆JAN VAN EYCK
Van Eyck was the greatest of the Flemish painters. Abandoning the fanciful decorative styles of late Gothic art, he represented people, things, and landscapes in a down-to-earth, realistic fashion, with minute attention to detail. He is first heard of at The Hague in 1422. From 1425 he worked in Bruges in the service of Philip III of Burgundy. He was employed in diplomatic activity, traveling widely. He died in Bruges in 1441. His works include *Madonna with the Canon Van der Paele* (1436), *Enthroned Madonna and Child* (1437), and *St. Barbara* (1437).

ROGIER ◆ VAN DER WEYDEN
Descent from the Cross, c.1435; oil on panel, 220 x 262 cm. (86.6 x 103 in.); Prado, Madrid.
Rogier van der Weyden was born in Tournai in 1399 or 1400 and died in Brussels in 1464. A pupil of Robert Campin, he was a painter of great imaginative power and religious intensity. Rogier's world, seemingly one of simple piety, is in fact highly dramatic and expressive.

◆ HEIRS
Left: Hieronymus Bosch, *Prodigal Son,* c.1510; oil on canvas, 70.6 cm. (27.8 in.) diameter; Boymans-van Beuningen Museum, Rotterdam.
Right: Hans Memling, *Reliquary of St. Ursula*, 1489 (detail); oil on panel, 87 x 91 x 33 cm. (34.25 x 35.8 x 13 in.); Hans Memling Museum, Bruges.
Bosch (c.1450-1516) and Memling (c.1435-94) exemplify the great variety of Flemish art.

◆ROBERT CAMPIN
St. Veronica, c.1430 (detail); panel, 144 x 53 cm. (48.5 x 21 in.); Städelscher Kunstinstitut, Frankfurt.
Robert Campin, also known as the Master of Flémalle, was born in Valenciennes in 1378-79 and died in Tournai in 1444.

OIL PAINTING

In his work as an artist, Van Eyck represented the real world so accurately, and with such technical mastery, that his paintings have been compared to mirrors that reflect every detail shown up by the light. It used to be claimed that he was the inventor of oil painting, but that is not quite correct. However, Flemish artists did improve on existing methods, employing linseed oil and turpentine which dried quickly. This enabled painters to produce effects that had previously been inconceivable. Working in oils, they could apply the paint more smoothly and precisely, obtaining brighter, more luminous coloring and greater tonal variety. Such changes made possible great advances in the rendering of light and the creation of lifelike images.

Presumed self-portrait of Van Eyck, *Man in a Turban*, 1433; oil on panel, 25.5 x 19 cm. (10 x 7.5 in.); National Gallery, London.

♦ FROM TEMPERA TO OIL
Until the 15th century, tempera was almost the only medium used in European painting. It consisted of ground-up pigments mixed with water and egg, sometimes with egg yolk only. Surfaces painted in tempera appear as areas of fairly uniform color. In the 15th century painters sought to develop richer colors, with a wider range from light to dark, and to achieve more subtle effects. The only way to do this was to replace the egg – or gum, or wax – in the pigment with oil. The passages between different colors were softened by the application of glazes, that is, by the laying on of successive layers of color to obtain the tonalities desired. Throughout much of the Renaissance paintings consisted of alternate glazes of tempera colors and oil colors. The technique of oil painting spread to Italy only in the second half of the 15th century, pioneered by Piero della Francesca, Antonello da Messina, and Leonardo da Vinci.

CARPENTRY ♦
The panels are held together with dove-tail joints and reinforced at the back with a criss-cross wooden frame.

VISITORS ♦
Two art patrons are received in Van Eyck's workshop where his many pupils and assistants are at work.

MANNEQUINS ♦
To provide models for the length of time needed to execute the work, mannequins with plaster garments are used.

A WORK IN ♦ PROGRESS
An assistant applies color glazes to Van Eyck's painting *The Madonna of Chancellor Rolin*, while two young pupils are drawing from the models. A workshop assistant prepares the colors.

♦ **JAN VAN EYCK**
The Madonna of Chancellor Rolin, c.1434; oil on panel, 66 x 62 cm. (26 x 23.6 in.); Louvre, Paris. Gift of the Chancellor of Burgundy (kneeling) to the cathedral of Autun.

♦**THE WINDOW**
A landscape is seen through the end wall. The positioning of the figures directs our gaze to the space beyond.

♦**THE LIGHTING**
A subtle play of light from many sources: the arches, the side windows, and even the decoration on the gold-rich garments.

THE MASTER ♦
The painter Jan van Eyck, sitting with his back to us, studies the features of a well-to-do lady whose portrait he is about to paint.

WOOD SAMPLES ♦
The panels on which the artist painted were made of oak, lime, beech, poplar, birch, or cedar. Barrel staves and the planks of demolished ships might be used.

BRUEGEL

Between 1560 and 1569 Pieter Bruegel the Elder executed a series of masterpieces showing scenes from peasant life. By doing so he established a new genre of painting, subsequently of great importance in the history of art. It was perhaps significant that during this decade the Low Countries rebelled against Spanish rule, and that the Duke of Alva, commanding a Spanish army, began a reign of terror. Bruegel portrayed the misery and horror of the events, as well as gross or festive scenes from ordinary life. What made him a Renaissance painter was his ability to place all this convincingly in the context of the natural world, that is, in real landscapes reflecting the changing seasons, and the lives and work of those who inhabited them. The faces, clothes, and gestures of ordinary folk are the prime subject of Bruegel's art.

Pieter Bruegel,
Self-portrait, c.1565
(detail);
drawing in pen and
brown ink,
25 x 21.6 cm.
(9.8 x 8.5 in.);
Albertina, Vienna.

♦ **PIETER BRUEGEL**
Pieter Bruegel was probably born in Breda, in Brabant, around 1525, though some sources do mention other places in both Brabant and Limburg. Bruegel is documented as an active artist in the mid-16th century, with drawings of landscapes that can be dated to 1552. In Antwerp he came into contact with artists working in the Italian Renaissance manner, which had little influence on him; his inspiration was derived above all from the Flemish tradition. Bruegel's artistic career had three strands: he was a draftsman, an engraver, and a painter.
Two early masterpieces, *Flemish Proverbs* and the *Battle Between Carnival and Lent,* date from 1559. *Children's Games* was painted in 1560. From 1563 he lived in Brussels. In 1564 his son Pieter the Younger was born; he became a painter in the style of his father. In 1568 another son, Jan, was born; he became a painter of still-lifes known as "Velvet Bruegel". Pieter Bruegel the Elder died in Brussels in 1569.

♦ **PERSPECTIVE**
The superimposed perspective lines show that the chaos of the scene is under artistic control. In fact, the lines act as a basis for the structure of the composition.

♦ **A GREAT NARRATIVE**
Pieter Bruegel the Elder, *Children's Games*, 1560 (whole above, detail right); oil on panel, 118 x 161 cm. (46.5 x 63.4 in.); Kunsthistorisches Museum, Vienna. Bruegel crowds a great many people and incidents into a single scene. His ability to enter into everyday life and record its telling details is remarkable. Scholars have put forward various interpretations of this painting, but whatever its ultimate, probably symbolic, meaning may be, the painter's mastery of depiction is indisputable.

♦EIGHTY-FOUR
GAMES
Pieter Bruegel
the Elder,
Children's Games,
six details.
The painting is a
compendium of
children's games,
eighty-four of which
are shown.
Bruegel grasped
that, for a child, a
game is not simply
amusement, but an
activity governed by
strict rules.
Illustrated here is
the classic game of
running with a hoop;
the image is repeated
to generate a sense
of movement.
Other traditional
games included are
piggyback riding
and whipping a top.
Children are also
shown playing
balancing games
on a horizontal bar.

BLOATED ABANDON ♦
Pieter Bruegel
the Elder, *The Land
of Cockaigne*, 1567; oil
on panel, 52 x 72 cm.
(20.5 x 28.3 in.);
Alte Pinakothek,
Munich. The delights
of the glutton's
paradise have lured
men of three social
classes – a peasant, a
soldier, and a priest –
under the Tree of
Plenty. An armed
nobleman sits under
a pie-covered roof,
while various edibles
wander about.

♦AN ORDERLY CROWD
Pieter Bruegel
the Elder,
Peasant Wedding,
c.1568 (whole above
and detail, above left);
oil on panel, 114 x
163 cm. (45 x 64 in.);
Kunsthistorisches
Museum, Vienna.
Like *Children's
Games*, this famous
work is also crammed
with people and
events and yet, in
spite of its enormous
richness, the scene
is far from being
cluttered or confused.

This is due to the
arrangement of the
figures, to the effect
of making the
painting recede
toward the back-
ground, and to the
movement of people,
both those pushing
their way in and those
in the foreground.
It is likely that
Bruegel painted his
own portrait in the
figure of the well-
dressed man at
the end of the table,
conversing with
a monk.

GERMANY

Printing from movable type was introduced in Germany during the mid-15th century and was an important factor in the spread of humanism. It was made possible by a number of earlier developments, notably the spread of block-printing, which entailed cutting pictures and text into a large single block of wood. Then, as paper became more widely available, the mechanical printing press was developed. The final step was the invention of movable type – wooden blocks, each of which was carved with a raised letter of the alphabet; the letters could be arranged in any required combinations to produce words on a page. Using this much more economical and flexible method, Johann Gutenberg printed his famous Bible in Mainz in 1455. Some years later, Martin Schongauer (died 1491) established a flourishing printing works in Colmar. In 1492 the young Dürer, the most famous German painter of his day, visited it and was received by Schongauer's brothers, who had inherited the firm.

Albrecht Dürer, *The Emperor Maximilian I,* 1519; oil on panel, 74 x 61.5 cm. (29 x 24.2 in.); Kunsthistorisches Museum, Vienna.

♦ GERMANY

In the 14th and 15th centuries Germany was a patchwork of independent states and cities. Princes or bishops ruled states of widely different sizes, while the cities, independent since the 14th century, had their own charters and were often grouped into leagues. Both states and cities were part of the Holy Roman Empire, but the Emperor had little real power, although the idea of the Empire inspired an almost religious veneration.

The cities were prosperous and population increased, but the unequal distribution of wealth caused tensions and revolts that were at times very violent, and were suppressed with even greater ferocity.

The accession of Charles V to the imperial throne coincided with the German Reformation, a protest against papal abuses that took on national and social as well as religious dimensions.

With the Reformation, patrons of the arts more often favored secular works, although paintings of religious subjects still found patrons in the courts of southern princes.

THE FORM ♦
The worker in charge of the form, the metal frame holding the two pages to be printed.

♦ THE SCHONGAUER WORKSHOP
The year is 1492. Martin Schongauer's brothers and their employees are busy at work, practicing the crafts of wood and copper engraving, making images that can be inked and printed and therefore reproduced in multiple copies.

The fame of this workshop spread throughout Europe. Among those who frequented it were professional carvers and contemporary artists eager to obtain study materials and learn new techniques.

THE ENGRAVING ♦
A craftsman accentuates the raised areas with a small knife. Another, with a hammer and chisel, cuts away the unnecessary parts of the block, which on the final engraving will show as white.

THE YOUNG DÜRER ♦
The artist makes a copy in ink on wood from an original drawing. From it the workshop will make a wood engraving.

INKS ♦
The preparation of the inks is entrusted to young apprentices. These boys are often the sons or grandsons of older workers who wish to pass on their craft to a family member. Even the sons of the workshop master must start with the humblest of jobs.

✦ COLMAR
The Schongauer workshop looked out onto a street in the German town of Colmar.

✦ TYPESETTING
Seated at the shallow box where the characters are kept, a typesetter makes up a page. A colleague in front of him measures the line he has composed with a type-stick.

✦ THE PRINTING PRESS
Ink is spread onto the blocks with cotton wads, while a clean sheet of paper is arranged on the form before being passed through the press.

✦ GERMANY
Many German cities were important artistic centers during the 15th and 16th centuries.

PAPER ✦
Next to a stack of blank paper are some printed proofs. They are checked by one of the Schongauer brothers.

WOOD SCULPTURE

South German wood sculpture of the late 15th century was a major European art. Its leading exponents – Tilman Riemenschneider, Hans Multscher, Michael Pacher, Michel Erhart, and Veit Stoss – are less famous now than the painters of their time. Yet they took to its highest point the creation of winged altarpieces, the Flügelaltar. These extraordinary works combining sculpture, painting, and architectural design were often enormous structures. The one made by Veit Stoss for St. Mary's Church in Cracow reached a height of 15 meters (about 50 feet). In the middle of this wonderful flight of fancy was a compartment holding sculptures, the corpus, which could be closed by folding in the two wings. On feast-days the wings were opened so that the figures inside could be admired.

♦ROUGH-CUTTING
A carpenter rough-cuts a figure from a piece of wood fixed to two beams with iron clamps. He is using a broad-bladed hatchet sharpened on one side only. He will also use other tools, including the narrow-bladed axe, sharpened on both sides, which lies beside him.

♦THE SHELL
The wooden figure is hollowed out inside. Lime paste and plaster are used to fill in any unsightly cracks in the wood and to make small repairs.

♦THE SURFACE
Many thin layers of plaster, glue, and hardening agents are applied to the surface of the statue. Alternatively, some areas are covered with fabric.

♦ POLISHING
When the surface is dry the statue is polished to make it smooth. It is then ready to be painted in bright colors.

THE WINGS ♦
The two hinged wings attached to the sides of the corpus were decorated with painted bas-reliefs both inside and out. They were opened only on feast-days or during special ceremonies.

♦ THE SUMMIT
The crowning superstructure is decorated with small figures, vine tendrils, shrubs, spirals, and finials in the flamboyant Gothic style.

♦ THE FIGURES
The free-standing figures are colorfully painted.

THE CORPUS ♦
This is the central element, the box containing the main subject of the altarpiece.

THE PREDELLA ♦
The predella, at the base, raised the central part of the altar, making it more visible. The theme of its decoration was subordinate to that represented in the corpus and wings.

Michel Erhart, *St. John the Evangelist*, c.1493 (details above and below); Monastery Church, Blaubeuren.

✦ CITIES OF THE WOOD CARVERS

The region where the most gifted wood carvers worked was the southern part of present-day Germany. This area was culturally homogeneous and contained many small and medium-sized cities. Some of them were imperial cities, with independent constitutions, not subject to the territorial states. The most important cities were Strasbourg, Freiburg, Basel, Ulm, Augsburg, Nuremberg, and Munich. Other cities were ecclesiastical possessions. Here, wood carvers could study and learn much, but their prospects of employment were limited because of the monopoly held by the cathedral workshop. The work done by carvers was not always on a large scale. Much of it consisted of small objects, such as candelabras that could be hung from the ceiling, statuettes, and objects used for domestic devotion.

✦ VEIT STOSS

Probably born in Nuremberg around 1450. Between 1477 and 1496 he lived in Cracow, where he ran a flourishing workshop that produced carvings for the court and for German merchants. It was during this period that he made the high altar for St. Mary's Church and many tombs, including one for Casimir IV of Poland (1492). On his return to Nuremberg a disastrous legal dispute greatly curtailed his activities. He nevertheless carved a number of altars, crucifixes, and statuettes, working in Nuremberg and other south German cities.

✦ THE BAMBERG ALTAR

High altar, 1520-23; wood sculpture, carpentry in firwood, carving in limewood, height 355 cm. (11 ft. 8 in.); Cathedral, Bamberg.

GERMAN PAINTERS

Soon after its woodcarving tradition reached a climax of Gothic splendor, Germany also produced several great painters: Matthias Grünewald, Albrecht Dürer, Lucas Cranach, Albrecht Altdorfer, and Hans Holbein the Younger. The greater part of their work was done in the first three decades of the 16th century, but the extent to which it can be related to the Italian Renaissance has long been a subject of debate – although Dürer's development certainly did owe a great deal to humanist influences and his study of antiquity. In any event, 16th-century German painting has its own distinct identity, manifested in its often turbulent emotional expressiveness and sense of inwardness. In its mainly religious preoccupations, it reflects the mood of German society before and during the Reformation.

♦ LUCAS CRANACH
Albrecht of Brandenburg Before the Crucifix, 1520-25; panel, 158 x 112 cm. (62 x 44 in.); Alte Pinakothek, Munich.
The artist was born in Kronach, in Upper Franconia, in 1472, and died in Weimar in 1553.
From 1505 he worked in the service of Frederick the Wise, Elector of Saxony. Among his most celebrated works are an earlier *Crucifixion* (1503), *Portrait of the Cuspinians* (1503), *Venus in a Landscape* (1529), and *The Expulsion of Frederick the Wise, Elector of Saxony* (1529).

♦ ALBRECHT ALTDORFER
Crucifixion, c.1520; panel, 75 x 57.5 cm. (29.5 x 22.6 in.); Museum of Art, Budapest.
The artist was born c.1480. His peculiarly expressive painting shows the influence of Cranach's early works. In 1510 he painted *The Holy Family Resting on the Flight into Egypt* and a *St. George*, in 1519 *Scenes of the Passion,* and in 1529 *Alexander's Victory.* He was a pioneer of landscape painting and produced many etchings and woodcuts. He died in Regensburg in 1538.

♦ PLAY OF ARCHES
Albrecht Dürer, *Adoration of the Magi*, 1504 (whole above and detail left); oil on panel, 100 x 114 cm. (39.4 x 45 in.); Uffizi, Florence.
In this painting by Dürer the setting is strictly constructed according to the principles of perspective, with the figures arranged as if on an ideal stage. But the most striking aspect of the work is the subtle interplay of the arches, whose meticulous detail and carefully angled placing underpin the structure of the painting.

♦ ADAM AND EVE
Albrecht Dürer, *Adam and Eve*, 1507; oil on panel, *Adam* 209 x 81 cm. (82.25 x 32 in.), *Eve* 209 x 83 cm. (82.25 x 32.7 in.); Prado, Madrid.
Dürer painted these two panels shortly after returning to Nuremberg from his second visit to Italy, where he had devoted himself to the study of perspective and sought to discover the ideal proportions of the human figure. They are the first examples of life-sized nudes in German painting. For Dürer, they represented the perfect proportions of the human body.

♦ DÜRER'S LAST WORKS
Albrecht Dürer, *Four Apostles*, 1526; oil on panel, 215.5 x 76 cm. (85 x 30 in.); Alte Pinakothek, Munich.
These two panels are Dürer's last monumental works, the final fruits of his artistic career.

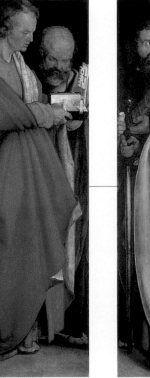

♦ **MATTHIAS GRÜNEWALD**
Crucifixion with Sts. Anthony and Sebastian, 1512-16; oil on panel, central panel 269 x 307 cm. (106 x 121 in.), side panels 237 x 76 cm. (93.3 x 30 in.); Unterlinden Museum, Colmar.
Grünewald was born between 1470 and 1480 and died in 1528.

His most celebrated work is the Isenheim altarpiece. The figures are distorted, the facial expressions are intense, and the colors are strikingly juxtaposed. The whole weight of Christ's body seems to hang from the cross and the tortured hands are opened in a spasm of pain.

♦ **TRIPTYCH**
Albrecht Dürer, *Nativity*, 1504; oil on panel, 155 x 126 cm. (61 x 49.5 in.); Alte Pinakothek, Munich.

The Paumgartner triptych consists of the Nativity flanked by the figures of St. George and St. Eustace.

FRANCE

Jean Fouquet, *Etienne Chevalier and St. Stephen* (detail of Chevalier, Charles VII's treasurer, above, and detail of St. Stephen below), 1447; panel, 95 x 85 cm. (37.5 x 33.5 in.); Staatliche Museen, Berlin.

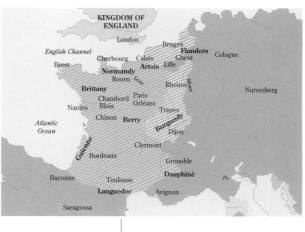

The exhausting Hundred Years' War between France and England ended in 1453, ushering in a period of renewed vigor for the French monarchy and the arts. The late-15th-century artist Jean Fouquet carried on the great tradition of the French miniaturists and also worked on a larger scale, becoming the greatest French portraitist and court painter of his time. Having spent several years in Rome during the papacy of Eugenius IV, Fouquet was certainly influenced by the revival of interest in classical antiquity and by the new theories of perspective. But it was in the early decades of the 16th century that there was a real flowering of Renaissance culture in France, partly thanks to thirty years of campaigning by French armies in Italy. The court of Francis I (especially after the arrival of Leonardo), the building of magnificent châteaux in the Loire Valley, the activities of the School of Fontainebleau, and the existence of painters such as Cousin, working in Paris, all reflected the influence of the Renaissance.

♦ **THE FRENCH MONARCHY**
At the end of the Hundred Years' War (1337-1453) France was unified under the House of Valois. In 1477, having expelled the English from all of France except the port of Calais, Louis XI (ruled 1461-86) took advantage of the death of Charles the Bold to recover the French territories of the duchy of Burgundy. His successors then began a policy of territorial expansion. In 1494 Charles VIII (1483-98) invaded Italy; in 1499 Louis XII (1498-1515) conquered the Duchy of Milan; and from 1520 Francis I (1515-47) initiated a long series of conflicts with the Emperor Charles V for the control of Italy and Flanders.

♦ **CHAMBORD**
In the woods to the east of Blois in the Loire Valley, Francis I built a château worthy of France's "New Monarchy" and splendid Renaissance court. Work on the château lasted from 1519 to 1550.

FRANCE UNDER ♦ THE VALOIS KINGS
The kingdom of France and the duchy of Burgundy.

♦ **THE CORNER TOWER**
Work is in progress to complete the left wing, and in particular the roof of the tower. For this, as for other tower roofs at Chambord, the characteristic "pepper-pot" design has been chosen.

THE COURTYARD ♦
When finished, the courtyard was used to receive or see off guests. It was also used as a riding-ground, and for tournaments, games, and open-air spectacles.

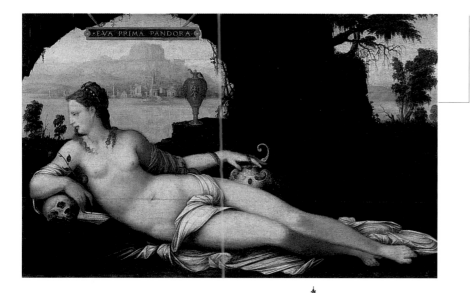

✦ COUSIN THE ELDER
Eve as Pandora,
c.1549; panel,
98 x 150 cm.
(38.5 x 59 in.);
Louvre, Paris.
Francis I employed
Italian, Flemish, and
French artists at
Fontainebleau, near
Paris. At the same
time, in Paris, Jean
Cousin (c.1490-c.1560)
was influenced by
engravers of the
Italian school and
developed his own
style.

✦ JEAN FOUQUET
*Portrait of the Clown
Gonnella*, before 1441;
tempera on panel,
36 x 24 cm.
(14.2 x 9.5 in.);
Kunsthistorisches
Museum, Vienna.
Jean Fouquet
(c.1420-c.1480)
visited Florence,
where he was struck
by Fra Angelico's
subtle treatment of
light and space.
He was also received
at the court of the
Este in Ferrara.

✦ MAIN BLOCK
The square central
part of the château
has a roof bristling
with spires, turrets,
cupolas, and tall
gables.

THE CANAL ✦
All the materials used
for building the
château were brought
to the site on barges
and pontoons along a
canal built specially
to connect the
château with the
nearby Loire River.

SPAIN

In 1492 the Moors were expelled from Spain, which became a single kingdom, and Christopher Columbus landed in the Americas. The Spanish sovereigns, Ferdinand and Isabella, patronized printers, encouraging the spread of humanism. Their successor, the Emperor Charles V, followed their example, and despite the oppressive religious climate under Philip II, Spanish culture enjoyed a golden age. During this period Spain, sustained by vast quantities of silver from the New World, was the dominant power in Europe. It was the age of the writer Miguel de Cervantes (1547-1616) and of El Greco, one of Spain's greatest painters.

Titian,
Portrait of Philip II,
1551; oil on canvas,
193 x 111 cm.
(76 x 43.75 in.);
Prado, Madrid.

✦ **THE NATION STATE**
The creation of the Spanish state went hand in hand with the gradual elimination of the Muslim kingdoms in the peninsula.
In 1469, the marriage of Ferdinand of Aragon (1479-1516) and Isabella of Castile (1474-1504) led to the unification of the two largest kingdoms of the Iberian peninsula.
In 1492, the long "Reconquest" ended when Ferdinand and Isabella conquered Granada, the last Moorish state in Spain.
Between 1516 and 1556 Spain was ruled by Charles I, better known as the Holy Roman Emperor Charles V.
Under Charles's son, Philip II (1556-98), Spain was the center of a European empire, including the Low Countries and much of Italy.
Moreover, between 1519 and 1533, the Spanish colonial empire had grown enormously with the conquest of Mexico and the destruction of the Inca empire in South America.
From 1530 onwards vast quantities of precious metals poured into Spain from the New World, financing Spanish intervention in the French civil wars and the attempted invasion of England by the Armada.

✦ **SPAIN IN THE MID-15TH CENTURY**
Until it was unified under Ferdinand and Isabella, Spain was divided between Castile, Navarre, Aragon, and Granada.

✦ **THE CARRACK**
This 3-masted ship, used as a merchant-man from the 15th century, was suitable for long voyages along the coasts from Spain to the Low Countries.

✦ **CARGOES**
Bales of wool and tobacco, ceramics, fabrics, and metal goods have been unloaded from the barge onto the quay. Barrels of oil and wine are being loaded into the boat.

♦ A THRONG OF FIGURES
El Greco, *Disrobing of Christ*, 1577-79; oil on canvas, 285 x 173 cm. (112 x 68 in.); Cathedral, Toledo. In this painting a dense throng of anonymous figures and faces crowds around and above the central figure of Christ.
El Greco abandons the Renaissance ideal of spatial depth in order to convey the sense of pressure caused by the crowd pressing in and pushing the figure of Christ toward the onlooker.

Self-portrait of El Greco, detail from *The Burial of Count Orgaz.*

♦ ADORATION
El Greco, *Adoration of the Name of Jesus*, 1597; oil on canvas, 140 x 110 cm. (55 x 43.3 in.); Monastery of San Lorenzo, Escorial, Madrid.

♦ EL GRECO
Domenikos Theotokopoulos (El Greco) was probably born in Candia, Crete, in 1541. In 1567 he arrived in Venice where he is believed to have been a pupil of Titian.
In his intense, haunting works, elements typical of Renaissance art blend with those of the Byzantine tradition, still very much alive in his native land. From 1576 he lived in Spain, initially in Madrid, where he was attracted by the prospect of work on the decoration of the Escorial, at that time the largest building project in Europe. He soon moved to Toledo, where he painted an altarpiece with *The Disrobing of Christ* for the new cathedral. In the ultra-religious climate of the Counter-Reformation he was criticized for placing Christ's head below the surrounding figures. Nonetheless, he received many commissions from churches and monasteries. In 1580 he painted *The Martyrdom of St. Maurice* for Philip II. As well as religious paintings, El Greco produced an extraordinary series of portraits. He died in Toledo in 1614.

♦ THE PORT
The port of Sanlùcar was situated at the mouth of the Guadalquivir River. It was an important link in the sea route to the inland city of Seville, the base for transatlantic voyages.

♦ WAREHOUSES AND DOCKYARDS
Merchandise passing through the port was stored in warehouses along the wharf. Dockyards were fitted out for the maintenance of boats and ships.

♦ THE TARTANE
A small single-masted sailing ship used for coastal trading. Its cargo of gun-carriages from Germany has just been unloaded.

♦ THE MIRACLE
El Greco, *The Burial of Count Orgaz*, 1586-88; oil on canvas, 140 x 340 cm. (55 x 134 in.); San Tomè, Toledo. The work celebrates the appearance of Sts. Stephen and Augustine at the count's funeral.

ENGLAND

For a long time England was relatively isolated, and Renaissance ideas were absorbed only slowly. The 16th century was a turbulent period in which the Church of England separated from Rome and there were political and social problems. Protestant zealotry led to the destruction of much older religious art, yet it was at this time that portrait painting emerged and flourished in England as nowhere else in Europe. Under Henry VIII and his court painter Hans Holbein, royal portraiture assumed a certain political importance as a form of propaganda. Under Elizabeth I, painting remained a minor art, despite the advent of a great miniaturist, Nicholas Hilliard. But in literature England produced a host of poets and playwrights, of whom one, William Shakespeare (1564-1616), was a supreme genius.

Hans Holbein the Younger, *Portrait of Nicholas Kratzer*, 1528; tempera on panel, 83 x 67 cm. (32.5 x 26.5 in.); Louvre, Paris.

♦ THE TUDORS
Henry VII was the first Tudor king of England (1485-1509). He came to the throne after defeating Richard III at the Battle of Bosworth Field which ended the Wars of the Roses (1455-85) between the Houses of York and Lancaster. Henry VII was succeeded by Henry VIII (ruled 1509-47), the husband of Catherine of Aragon. Because Pope Clement VII refused to grant the divorce that would have allowed the English king to marry Ann Boleyn (later beheaded), Henry VIII broke away from the Roman Catholic Church. On this issue he clashed violently with his chancellor Sir Thomas More, who was executed in 1535. After the short reigns of Edward VI and Mary I, the crown passed to Elizabeth I (1558-1603).
Below: Hans Holbein the Younger, *Thomas More*, 1527 (detail); pen and ink on paper, 38.7 x 52.4 cm. (15.25 x 20.5 in.); Kunstmuseum, Basel.

♦ HANS HOLBEIN THE YOUNGER
Portrait of Henry VIII, 1536-37; tempera on panel, 28 x 19 cm. (11 x 7.5 in.); Thyssen Collection, Lugano.
Holbein was born in Augsburg in 1497-98 and died of plague in London in 1543. He executed brilliant, astonishingly realistic portraits of Henry VIII, his courtiers, and leading figures in English society.

♦ THE UNIVERSITY OF OXFORD
In the great university library an astronomy lesson is in progress. The main reading-room has a vaulted ceiling with Gothic ribbing, while the adjoining room has a trussed roof.

♦ NICHOLAS HILLIARD
Young Man Leaning against a Tree, 1588; watercolor, 13.5 x 7.3 cm. (5.25 x 2.8 in.); Victoria and Albert Museum, London.
The most celebrated miniature painted by Hilliard (c.1547-1619). A young lover is surrounded by roses – and thorns.

♦ THE GLOBE
Having recognized
that the Earth was
round, scientists now
formed theories
about its geography.

♦ NICHOLAS KRATZER
The court astronomer
shows his scientific
instruments to an
attentive audience.

♦ HANS HOLBEIN
The artist studies
Nicholas Kratzer as
he speaks, for the
portrait he is painting.

♦ THE AUDIENCE
Teachers and
students engage in
a lively debate after
every lesson.

THE ASTROLABE ♦
This instrument
indicates the position
of the stars and
measures the
distance in degrees
between them.

♦ KEY DATES IN THE HISTORY OF THE RENAISSANCE

1401 In a competition for the execution of the bronze door of the Florence Baptistery, Filippo Brunelleschi produces a work that embodies innovations later seen as characteristic of the Italian Renaissance.

1416 Donatello carves and exhibits his statue of *St. George* in Orsanmichele. Florentine sculpture begins to show a preoccupation with the precise rendering of reality.

1425 Florentine painting follows the example of sculpture. Masaccio uses linear perspective to paint the Brancacci Chapel frescoes in the Church of the Carmine.

1434 The representation of space also characterizes Flemish art. Van Eyck paints his *Giovanni Arnolfini and his Wife* and Van der Weyden, a year later, *Descent from the Cross*.

1453 The end of the Hundred Years' War between England and France, which, like Spain, are unwittingly about to enter the age of world exploration. Germany and Italy remain patchworks of smaller states.

1454 The Peace of Lodi establishes peace between the five largest states in Italy, and this leads to a forty-year period of tranquillity, creating a situation favorable to the flourishing of art and culture.

1460 Piero della Francesca paints the *Flagellation* in Urbino. His work has a strong influence on the artists of central and northern Italy.

1474 The achievements of Donatello and Masaccio in Florence are absorbed by Andrea Mantegna, who has just finished the frescoes of the Camera Picta in the Ducal Palace of Mantua.

1475 The Venetian artist Giovanni Bellini meets Antonello da Messina, assimilates Flemish innovations, and with Mantegna becomes the greatest painter of northern Italy.

1492 The discovery of America marks the beginning of a new era. The last Moorish kingdom in Spain falls. Lorenzo the Magnificent, the personification of the Renaissance, dies in Florence.

1494 Charles VIII of France invades Italy and this begins a period of wars in Italy. It will end only in the middle of the 16th century with the establishment of Spanish rule.

1497 Leonardo da Vinci finishes painting the *Last Supper* in the refectory of the Convent of Santa Maria delle Grazie.

1504 Leonardo, Michelangelo, and Raphael live and work for a brief period in Florence. The *David* is finished and the first studies are made for the *Mona Lisa*. In Germany, Albrecht Dürer paints *The Adoration of the Magi*.

1508 In Venice, at about this time, Giorgione paints *The Tempest*. In Rome Michelangelo begins to paint the ceiling of the Sistine Chapel and Raphael works on the Vatican Stanze.

1516 In Germany, Grünewald paints the *Crucifixion with Saints Anthony and Sebastian*. In Venice Titian finishes painting the *Assumption of the Virgin*. Leonardo moves to the court of the French king Francis I.

1517 In Germany, Martin Luther nails 95 theses to the church door at Wittenberg, attacking religious abuses. The Protestant Reformation has begun.

1534 The English Parliament recognizes Henry VIII as head of the Church of England, separated from Rome. During Henry's reign the art of secular portrait-painting spreads.

1550 The Loire Valley is now an important artistic center. Work is finished on the château of Chambord, which Francis I builds as the symbol of new cultural values inspired by the Italian Renaissance.

1559 The Peace of Cateau-Cambrésis ends the long Franco-Spanish wars. Italy now moves into the age of the Counter-Reformation.

1577 El Greco paints *The Disrobing of Christ*. El Greco is the most important painter at the court of Philip II, who has succeeded the Emperor Charles V as the king of Spain.

♦ RENAISSANCE HISTORIOGRAPHY

The word "Renaissance" is commonly used to refer to the historical period lasting from about 1400 to 1600. In European history this period falls between the Middle Ages and the Modern Age.

EARLY HISTORIOGRAPHY

Full-scale studies of the Renaissance as a cultural phenomenon are relatively recent, despite the fact that people living at the time had hailed their epoch as one in which learning had been revived and the arts reborn. In addition to the humanists of the 14th and 15th centuries, the art historian and painter Giorgio Vasari (1511-1574) played a pioneering role in this self-definition. In his *Lives of the Most Excellent Painters, Sculptors, and Architects* (1550), Vasari claimed that the arts in Italy, and especially Florence, had reached "the height of perfection", stimulated by the rediscovery of classical culture. Understandably, Vasari has been regarded as the founder of Renaissance studies, and many of his critical and interpretative concepts are still of value. However, his opinion was slanted in some important respects. Though born in Arezzo, he was a Florentine by training, and became a friend of the Grand Duke Cosimo de' Medici. As a consequence, he exalted the art of the Florentines and tended to relegate the achievements of the Venetian and other schools to a secondary place. Vasari made another, more indirect, contribution to Renaissance studies. Commissioned by the Grand Duke in 1560, he drew up the plans for a building whose ground floor was intended to house the administrative offices of the Florentine state; hence its name, the Uffizi ("Offices"). The Medici art collection was moved into the building, which eventually became one of the world's great public museums and a great treasure-house of Renaissance art.

RECENT HISTORIOGRAPHY

Modern Renaissance studies began in the 19th century, largely thanks to the publication of *The Civilization of the Renaissance in Italy* (1860) by the Swiss historian Jacob Burckhardt. For a long time after this, following the examples of Vasari and Burckhardt, historians continued to write about the Renaissance in Italian terms, describing its "arrival" in other countries as an import from Italy. But twentieth-century writers have taken much wider views of the period. Art historians have studied the achievements of the Flemish school and the works created for leading European courts, and as a result they now stress the independent nature of some developments and the two-way nature of the traffic between northern Europe and Italy.

Also cultural historians no longer interpret the Renaissance solely in terms of a "rebirth", but have identified some fundamental elements in the outlook of Renaissance people, expressed in attitudes toward time, death, and poverty. In contrast to the Middle Ages, when the passage of time was seen in religious terms as the unfolding of a divinely ordained drama, the Renaissance conceived of time primarily as a factor in worldly affairs such as political planning and economic processes. Attitudes to death were also profoundly modified. In the Middle Ages, death was not thought of as terrible in itself, but as a preliminary to judgement by God. Renaissance men and women, like their admired predecessors in antiquity, felt keenly the transitory nature of life, craved fame and remembrance, and feared death and oblivion. Finally, for much of the Middle Ages a poor man was seen as the image of Christ. Poverty was felt to possess a certain dignity, and to help rather than hinder the pursuit of righteousness. By contrast, from the Renaissance onward wealth and worldly succes swere regarded as admirable in themselves, justly rewarding ability and virtue. Understood in this context, the Renaissance becomes a more complex, but also a more dynamic and fascinating concept.

♦ LIST OF WORKS INCLUDED IN THIS BOOK

(Works reproduced in their entirety are indicated with the letter E; those of which only a detail is featured are followed by the letter D.)

The works reproduced in this book are listed here, with their date (when known), the place where they are currently housed, and the page number. The numbers in bold type refer to the credits on page 64.

Abbreviations: APM, Alte Pinakothek, Munich; BM, Brera, Milan; BMF, Bargello Museum, Florence; KMV, Kunsthistorisches Museum, Vienna; NGL, National Gallery, London; VR, Vatican, Rome.

ANONYMOUS
1. *Belvedere Apollo,* 2nd century A.D., marble (VR) 9 E; **2.** Cameo with portrait of Lodovico il Moro (Museo degli Argenti, Florence) 27 E; **3.** *Emperor Claudius,* first half of the 1st century A.D., marble (VR) 30 E; **4.** *Ideal City,* late 15th century, tempera on panel, 67.5 x 239 cm. (Galleria Nazionale delle Marche, Urbino) 21 E; **5.** *Laocoön,* 1st century A.D., marble (Cortile del Belvedere, VR) 30 E; **6.** *Rabbit-Hunting with a Ferret,* c.1560, tapestry, 300 x 360 cm. (M.H.D. Young Memorial Museum, San Francisco) 42 D; **7.** *Section of the dome of Florence Cathedral,* c.1440, drawing 10 E; **8.** *The Nile,* Hellenistic statue, marble (Cortile del Belvedere, VR) 30 E; **9.** *Venus Felix,* marble (Cortile Ottagono, VR) 31 E; **10.** *View of Rome After the Building of Sixtus V in 1602,* engraving (Raccolta Stampe Archivio Bertarelli, Milan) 30-31 E
ALTDORFER, ALBRECHT
11. *Crucifixion,* c.1520, oil on gold base on panel, 75 x 57.5 cm. (Museum of Art, Budapest) 54 E
ANDREA DEL CASTAGNO
12. *Last Supper,* 1447, fresco, 470 x 975 cm. (Convent of Sant'Apollonia, Florence) 17 E
ANGELICO, FRA
13. *Annunciation,* c.1438, fresco, 230 x 321 cm. (Monastery of San Marco, Florence) 16 E; **14.** *St. Dominic at the Foot of the Cross,* 1442, fresco, 237 x 125 cm. (Monastery of San Marco, Florence) 16 E
ANTONELLO DA MESSINA
15. *Annunciation,* 1475, oil on panel, 45 x 34.5 cm. (Galleria Nazionale, Palermo) 37 E; **16.** *Condottiere,* 1475, oil on panel, 35 x 28 cm. (Louvre, Paris) 39 E; **17.** *Self-portrait,* 1473, oil on panel, 35.5 x 25.5 cm. (NGL) 37 E
BELLINI, GENTILE
18. *Procession of the Relic of the True Cross,* 1496, oil on canvas, 367 x 745 cm. (Accademia, Venice) 39 E
BELLINI, GIOVANNI
19. *Dead Christ Supported by Mary and St. John the Evangelist (Pietà),* c.1467, tempera on panel, 86 x 107 cm. (BM) 38 E, D; **20.** *Dead Christ Supported by Two Angels (Pietà),* c.1452, panel, 74 x 50 cm. (Correr Museum, Venice) 38 E; **21.** *Greek Madonna,* c.1475, tempera on panel, 84 x 62 cm. (BM) 38 E; **22.** *Madonna and Child,* 1508, oil on canvas, 85 x 115 cm. (BM) 39 E; **23.** *Polyptych of St. Vincent Ferrer,* before 1464, panel (Church of SS Giovanni e Paolo, Venice) 38 E; **24.** *Portrait of a Man,* 1480-90, panel, 32.8 x 25.5 cm. (Louvre, Paris) 39 E; **25.** *Portrait of Doge Loredan,* c.1501, oil on panel, 62 x 45 cm. (NGL) 36 E; **26.** San Giobbe altarpiece, c.1478, panel, 471 x 258 cm. (Accademia, Venice) 39 E, D
BEMBO, BONIFACIO
27. *Portrait of Bianca Maria Sforza,* 1460, tempera on canvas, 49 x 31 cm. (BM) 26 E; **28.** *Portrait of Francesco Sforza,* 1460, tempera on canvas, 49 x 31 cm. (BM) 26 E
BOSCH, HIERONYMUS
29. *Prodigal Son,* c.1510, oil on canvas, diameter 70.6 cm. (Boymans-van Beuningen Museum, Rotterdam) 45 E
BOTTICELLI, SANDRO
30. *Birth of Venus,* c.1483-85, tempera on canvas, 172 x 278 cm. (Uffizi, Florence) 17 E
BRUEGEL, PIETER THE ELDER
31. *Children's Games,* 1560, oil on panel, 118 x 161 cm. (KMV) 48 E, D, 49 D; **32.** *Peasant Wedding,* c.1568, oil on panel, 114 x 163 cm. (KMV) 49 E, D; **33.** *Self-portrait,* c.1565, drawing in pen and brown ink, 25 x 21.6 cm. (Albertina, Vienna) 48 D; **34.** *The Land of Cockaigne,* 1567, oil on panel, 52 x 72 cm. (APM) 49 E
BRUNELLESCHI, FILIPPO
35. *Sacrifice of Isaac,* panel for a door of Florence Baptistery, 1401, bronze relief (BMF) 12 E
CAMPIN, ROGER
36. *St. Veronica,* c.1430, tempera on panel, 144 x 53 cm. (Städelscher Kunstinstitut, Frankfurt) 45 D; **37.** *Virgin and Child Before a Firescreen,* 1420-25, tempera on panel, 63 x 48 cm. (NGL) 44 E
CARPACCIO, VITTORE
38. *Arrival of the Ambassadors of Britain at the Court of Brittany,* from the *Stories of St. Ursula,* 1490-96, tempera on panel, 275 x 589 cm. (Accademia, Venice) 7 E
COUSIN, JEAN THE ELDER
39. *Eve as Pandora,* c.1549, panel, 98 x 150 cm. (Louvre, Paris) 57 E
CRANACH, LUCAS THE ELDER
40. *Albrecht of Brandenburg Before the Crucifix,* 1520-25, panel, 158 x 112 cm. (APM) 54 E
DOMENICO VENEZIANO (DOMENICO DI BARTOLOMEO)
41. *Annunciation,* from the St. Lucy altarpiece, 1445-47, tempera on panel, 27.3 x 54 cm. (Fitzwilliam Museum, Cambridge, England) 18 E; **42.** *Madonna and Child with St. Francis, St. John the Baptist, St. Zenobius and St. Lucy,* from the St. Lucy altarpiece, 1445-47, tempera on panel, 209 x 216 cm. (Uffizi, Florence) 18 E, D; **43.** *Martyrdom of St. Lucy,* from the St. Lucy altarpiece, 1445-47, tempera on panel, 25 x 28.5 cm. (Gemäldegalerie, Berlin) 18 E; **44.** *Miracle of St. Zenobius,* from the St. Lucy altarpiece, 1445-47, tempera on panel, 28.6 x 32.5 cm. (Fitzwilliam Museum, Cambridge, England) 18 E; **45.** *St. Francis Receives the Stigmata,* from the St. Lucy altarpiece, 1445-47, tempera on panel, 26.7 x 30.5 cm. (National Gallery of Art, Washington, DC) 18 E; **46.** *St. John the Baptist in the Desert,* from the St. Lucy altarpiece, 1445-47, tempera on panel, 28.3 x 32.4 cm. (National Gallery of Art, Washington, DC) 18 E
DONATELLO (DONATO DI NICCOLO DI BETTO BARDI)
47. *Feast of Herod,* 1427, bronze relief (Church of San Giovanni, Siena) 13 E; **48.** *St. George,* 1415-16, marble, height 378 cm. (BMF) 12 E, D
DÜRER, ALBRECHT
49. *Adam,* 1507, oil on panel, 209 x 81 cm. (Prado, Madrid) 54 E; **50.** *Adoration of the Magi,* 1504, oil on panel, 100 x 114 cm. (Uffizi, Florence) 54 E, D; **51.** *Eve,* 1507, oil on panel, 209 x 83 cm. (Prado, Madrid) 54 E; **52.** *Four Apostles,* 1526, oil on panel, 215.5 x 76 cm. (APM) 54 E; **53.** *Nativity,* 1504, oil on panel, 155 x 126 cm. (APM) 55 E; **54.** *Self-portrait,* 1500, oil on panel, 67 x 49 cm. (APM) 55 E; **55.** *The Emperor Maximilian I,* 1519, oil on panel, 74 x 61.5 cm. (KMV) 50 E
ERHART, MICHEL
56. *St. John the Evangelist,* c.1493, wood sculpture (Monastery Church, Blaubeuren) 53 D
EYCK, HUBERT AND JAN VAN
57. *The Adoration of the Lamb,* 1420-32, oil on panel, 137.7 x 242.3 cm. (Cathedral of St. Bavon, Ghent) 44 E, D
EYCK, JAN VAN
58. *Giovanni Arnolfini and his Wife,* 1434, oil on panel, 82 x 60 cm. (NGL) 45 E, D; **59.** *Man in a Turban,* 1433, oil on panel, 25.5 x 19 cm. (NGL) 46 E; **60.** *Portrait of Margaret van Eyck,* 1439, oil on panel, 41.2 x 34.6 cm. (Groeningemuseum, Bruges) 45 D; **61.** *The Madonna of Chancellor Rolin,* c.1434, oil on panel, 66 x 62 cm. (Louvre, Paris) 47 E, D
FOUQUET, JEAN
62. *Etienne Chevalier and St. Stephen,* 1447, tempera on panel, 95 x 85 cm. (Staatliche Museen, Berlin) 56 D; **63.** *Portrait of the Clown Gonnella,* before 1441, tempera on panel, 36 x 24 cm. (KMV) 57 E
GHIBERTI, LORENZO
64. *Sacrifice of Isaac,* panel for a door of Florence Baptistery, 1401, bronze relief (BMF) 12 E; **65.** *St. John the Baptist,* 1412-16, bronze, height 254 cm. (Orsanmichele, Florence) 13 E; **66.** *St. Matthew,* 1419-22, bronze, height 270 cm. (Orsanmichele, Florence) 13 E, D
GHIRLANDAIO (DOMENICO BIGORDI)
67. *Angel Appearing to Zacharias,* 1490, fresco, 250 x 450 cm. (Tornabuoni Chapel, Santa Maria Novella, Florence) 9 D; **68.** *Miracle of the French Notary's Child,* 1480, fresco (Sassetti Chapel, Santa Trinita, Florence) 17 E
GIORGIONE
69. *Enthroned Madonna and Child,* 1504-5, panel, 200 x 152 cm. (San Liberale, Castelfranco Veneto) 40 E; **70.** *The Tempest,* c.1506, oil on canvas, 82 x 73 cm. (Accademia, Venice) 40 E, D; **71.** *The Three Philosophers,* 1508, oil on canvas, 123.5 x 144.5 cm. (KMV) 40 D
GRECO, EL
72. *Adoration of the Name of Jesus,* 1597, oil on canvas, 140 x 110 cm. (Monastery of San Lorenzo, Escorial, Madrid) 59 E; **73.** *Disrobing of Christ,* 1577-79, oil on canvas, 285 x 173 cm. (Cathedral, Toledo) 59 E; **74.** *The Burial of Count Orgaz,* 1586-88, oil on canvas, 140 x 340 cm. (Church of San Tomè, Toledo) 59 E, D
GRÜNEWALD, MATTHIAS
75. *Crucifixion with Sts. Anthony and Sebastian,* 1512-16, oil on panel, central panel 269 x 307 cm., side panels 237 x 76 cm. (Unterlinden Museum, Colmar) 55 E, D
HILLIARD, NICHOLAS
76. *Young Man Leaning Against a Tree,* 1588, watercolor, 13.5 x 7.3 cm. (Victoria and Albert Museum, London) 60 E
HOLBEIN, HANS THE YOUNGER
77. *Portrait of Erasmus of Rotterdam,* 1523, tempera on panel, 43 x 33 cm. (Louvre, Paris) 55 E; **78.** *Portrait of Henry VIII,* 1536-37, tempera on panel, 28 x 19 cm. (Thyssen Collection, Lugano) 60 E; **79.** *Portrait of Nicholas Kratzer,* 1528, tempera on panel, 83 x 67 cm. (Louvre, Paris) 60 E; **80.** *The Ambassadors,* 1533, tempera on panel, 207 x 209 cm. (NGL) 7 E; **81.** *Thomas More,* 1527, pen and ink on paper, 38.7 x 52.4 cm. (Kunstmuseum, Basel) 60 D
LEONARDO DA VINCI
82. *Mona Lisa,* 1505-14, oil on panel, 77 x 53 cm. (Louvre, Paris) 28 E, 29 D; **83.** *The Last Supper,* 1495-97, tempera on wall, 460 x 880 cm. (Refectory, Santa Maria delle Grazie, Milan) 26 E
LIPPI, FILIPPINO
84. *Adoration of the Magi,* 1496, oil on panel, 258 x 243 cm. (Uffizi, Florence) 16 E
LIPPI, FILIPPO
85. *Madonna and Child with the Birth of the Virgin,* 1452, panel, diameter 135 cm. (Pitti Palace, Florence) 16 E
MANTEGNA, ANDREA
86. Camera Picta, 1465-74, frescoes (Ducal Palace, Mantua) 25 D
MASACCIO (TOMMASO DI SER GIOVANNI DI MONE CASSAI)
87. *Expulsion,* 1425, fresco, 214 x 90 cm. (Brancacci Chapel, Santa Maria del Carmine, Florence) 14 E; **88.** *St. Peter Baptizing the Neophytes,* 1425, fresco, 247 x 172 cm. (Brancacci Chapel, Santa Maria del Carmine, Florence) 15 E, D; **89.** *St. Peter Healing with His Shadow,* 1426-27, fresco, 232 x 162 cm. (Brancacci Chapel, Santa Maria del Carmine, Florence) 15 E, D; **90.** *The Distribution of the Goods of the Community and the Death of Ananias,* 1426-27, fresco, 232 x 157 cm. (Brancacci Chapel, Santa Maria del Carmine, Florence) 15 E, D; **91.** *The Raising of the Son of Theophilus,* 1427-28, fresco, 230 x 598 cm. (Brancacci Chapel, Santa Maria del Carmine, Florence) 14 D; **92.** *The Tribute Money,* 1425, fresco, 247 x 597 cm. (Brancacci Chapel, Santa Maria del Carmine, Florence) 14 E, D; **93.** *The Trinity,* 1426-28, fresco, 640 x 317 cm. (Santa Maria di Novella, Florence) 14 E
MEMLING, HANS
94. *Arrival of St. Ursula in Cologne,* detail of the *Reliquary of St. Ursula,* 1489, oil on panel, 87 x 91 x 33 cm. (Hans Memling Museum, Bruges) 45 D
MICHELANGELO BUONARROTI
95. *David,* 1501-4, marble, height 410 cm. (Accademia, Florence) 28 E, 29 D; **96.** *Delphic Sibyl,* 1511, fresco, 395 x 380 cm. (Sistine Chapel, VR) 32 E; **97.** *Libyan Sibyl,* 1511, fresco, 395 x 380 cm. (Sistine Chapel, VR) 32 E; **98.** *Moses,* 1515, marble, height 235 cm. (San Pietro in Vincoli, Rome) 32 E; **99.** *Prophets* of the Sistine Chapel, 1511, fresco (Sistine Chapel, VR) 32 E, 33 E; **100.** Tomb of Julius II, 1515, marble (San Pietro in Vincoli, Rome) 32 E
NANNI DI BANCO, ANTONIO
101. *Four Crowned Martyrs,* c.1410-12, marble, life-size (Orsanmichele, Florence) 13 E
PIERO DELLA FRANCESCA
102. *Annunciation,* c.1470, oil and tempera on panel, 122 x 194 cm. (Galleria Nazionale dell'Umbria, Perugia) 11 D; **103.** *Baptism of Christ,* 1448-54, tempera on panel, 167 x 116 cm. (NGL) 19 E, D; **104.** *Flagellation,* c.1460, oil and tempera on panel, 59 x 81.5 cm. (Galleria Nazionale delle Marche, Urbino) 20 E, D; **105.** *Madonna and Child with Saints,* 1472-74, oil and panel, 248 x 170 cm. (BM) 19 E; **106.** *Montefeltro Diptych, Portrait of Battista Sforza, Portrait of Federico da Montefeltro,* 1465, oil on panel, 47 x 33 cm. (Uffizi, Florence) 20 E
POLLAIUOLO, ANTONIO
107. *St. Sebastian,* 1475, tempera on panel, 292 x 203 cm. (NGL) 17 E
PONTORMO, JACOPO
108. *Cosimo the Elder,* c.1518, oil on panel, 86 x 65 cm. (Uffizi, Florence) 10 D
RAPHAEL
109. *Disputation over the Sacrament,* c.1509, fresco, base 770 cm. (VR) 34 E; **110.** *Galatea,* 1511, fresco, 295 x 225 cm. (Villa Farnesina, Rome) 31 E; **111.** *Liberation of St. Peter from Prison,* 1513, fresco, base 660 cm. (VR) 35 E; **112.** *Madonna of the Goldfinch,* 1507, oil on panel, 107 x 77 cm. (Uffizi, Florence) 34 E; **113.** *Portrait of Angelo Doni,* c.1506, oil on panel, 63 x 45 cm. (Pitti Palace, Florence) 28 E, 29 D; **114.** *Portrait of Leo X,* 1516-19, tempera on panel, 154 x 119 cm. (Uffizi, Florence) 30 D; **115.** *Self-portrait,* 1506, oil on panel, 43 x 53 cm. (Uffizi, Florence) 34 E; **116.** *The School of Athens,* c.1510, fresco, base 770 cm. (VR) 6 D; 34 E, D, 35 D
STOSS, VEIT
117. *High Altar,* 1520-23, wood sculpture, carpentry in firwood, carving in limewood, height 355 cm. (Cathedral, Bamberg) 53 E, D
TITIAN
118. *Assumption of the Virgin,* 1516-18, oil on panel, 690 x 360 cm. (Church of Santa Maria Gloriosa dei Frari, Venice) 41 E; **119.** *Charles V on Horseback,* 1548, oil on canvas, 332 x 279 cm. (Prado, Madrid) 41 E; **120.** *Danaë,* 1553-54, oil on canvas, 128 x 178 cm. (Prado, Madrid) 41 E; **121.** *Pope Paul III with Alessandro and Ottavio Farnese,* 1546, oil on canvas, 210 x 174 cm. (Capodimonte Gallery, Naples) 41 E; **122.** *Portrait of Philip II,* 1551, oil on canvas, 193 x 111 cm. (Prado, Madrid) 58 E; **123.** *Self-portrait,* 1565-70, oil on canvas, 86 x 65 cm. (Prado, Madrid) 41 E
TURA, COSIMO
124. *Madonna Enthroned with Musician Angels,* c.1480, oil on panel, 239 x 101 cm. (NGL) 22 D, 23 E; **125.** *Spring,* c.1460, oil on panel, 116.2 x 101 cm. (NGL) 23 E
UCCELLO, PAOLO (PAOLO DI DONO)
126. *Battle of San Romano,* 1456, tempera on panel, 182 x 317 cm. (NGL) 7 E; **127.** *Miracle of the Host,* 1465-69, tempera on panel, 43 x 351 cm. (Galleria Nazionale delle Marche, Urbino) 19 D
VERROCCHIO (ANDREA DI FRANCESCO DI CIONE)
128. *Head of St. Jerome,* c.1460, tempera on paper glued on panel, 49 x 46 cm. (Pitti Palace, Florence) 16 D
WEYDEN, ROGIER VAN DER
129. *Descent from the Cross,* c.1435, oil on panel, 220 x 262 cm. (Prado, Madrid) 45 E

♦ INDEX

♦ CREDITS

The original and previously unpublished illustrations in this book were created at the request of, and by, DoGi s.r.l., who holds the copyright.

ILLUSTRATIONS: Simone Boni (50-51, 60-61); Lorenzo Cecchi (20-21, 36-37, 58-59); Boni-Cecchi (56-57); L. R. Galante (4-5, 6-7, 8-9, 24-25, 52-53); L.R. Galante-Manuela Cappon (42-43, 46-47); L. R. Galante-Francesco Petracchi (10-11, 22-23, 26-27)
Maps: Luca Cascioli (7 r, 8 c, 20 r, 42 c, 51 b, 56 r, 58 r)
Views: Lorenzo Cecchi and Francesco Petracchi: 11 r, 23 l, 36 c)
COVER: L. R. Galante
BACK COVER: L. R. Galante
FRONTISPIECE: L. R. Galante-Manuela Cappon

REPRODUCTIONS OF ARTISTS' WORKS:
ALTE PINAKOTHEK, MUNICH: 40, 52, 54; ARCHIVIO ALINARI, FLORENCE: 22, 85, 106, 113, 114, 127; ARCHIVIO ALINARI/GIRAUDON, FLORENCE, PARIS: 18, 19, 26, 38, 57,

73, 74, 79, 120, 122, 123, 129; ARCHIVIO ALINARI/GIRAUDON/LAUROS, FLORENCE, PARIS: 15, 16, 39, 61; ARCHIVIO DoGi, FLORENCE: 7, 12, 20, 47, 48, 56, 58, 64, 65, 66, 69, 83, 84, 98, 100, 126, 110, 117, 121; ARCHIVIO DoGi (FOTO SAPORETTI): 10; ARCHIVIO DoGi (QUATTRONE): 13, 14, 35, 42, 67, 68, 86, 87, 88, 89, 90, 91, 92, 93, 95, 101, 112, 115, 128; ARCHIVIO SCALA, FLORENCE: 23, 34, 72, 82, 111; BOYMANS-VAN BEUNINGEN MUSEUM, ROTTERDAM: 29; BRERA, MILAN: 105; THE BRIDGEMAN ART LIBRARY, LONDON: 4, 11, 21, 25, 27, 30, 31, 32, 41, 53, 70, 75, 76, 80, 104, 109, 118; ERIC LESSING, VIENNA: 24, 33, 63, 78; FITZWILLIAM MUSEUM, CAMBRIDGE, ENGLAND: 44; GALLERIA NAZIONALE DELL'UMBRIA, PERUGIA: 102; GEMÄLDEGALERIE, BERLIN: 43; GROENINGEMUSEUM, BRUGES: 60; HANS MEMLING MUSEUM, BRUGES: 94; JORG P. ANDERS PHOTO, BERLIN: 62; KUNSTHISTORISCHES MUSEUM, VIENNA: 55, 71; KUNSTMUSEUM, BASEL: 81; M.H.D. YOUNG MEMORIAL MUSEUM, SAN FRANCISCO: 6; MUSEO DEGLI ARGENTI, FLORENCE: 2; NATIONAL GALLERY, LONDON: 17, 37, 59, 103, 107, 124, 125; NATIONAL GALLERY OF ART, WASHINGTON: 45, 46; PRADO, MADRID: 49, 51, 119; RMN, PARIS: 77; STÄDELSCHER KUNSTINSTITUT, FRANKFURT: 36; THYSSEN

COLLECTION, LUGANO 77; UFFIZI, FLORENCE: 50, 108; VATICAN, ROME: 1, 3, 5, 8, 9, 96, 97, 99, 116.
COVER (clockwise, from top left): ARCHIVIO ALINARI: a, f, m, p, r; ARCHIVIO ALINARI/GIRAUDON: b; ARCHIVIO ALINARI/GIRAUDON/LAUROS: h, q; ARCHIVIO DoGi: g, k, t, v; ARCHIVIO DoGi (QUATTRONE): j, u, w, x; THE BRIDGEMAN ART LIBRARY: d, e, i, n, o; ERIC LESSING: l; NATIONAL GALLERY, LONDON: c, s
BACK COVER: ARCHIVIO DoGi, FLORENCE; MUSEO DEGLI ARGENTI, FLORENCE
DOCUMENTS
Abbreviations: a = above, b = below, c = center, r = right, l = left.
ARCHIVIO DoGi 10 al, b; 11 ar; 24 al, bl, ar; 30 al, c, ar, br; 31, al, ar, bl, br, c; ARCHIVIO DoGi (MARCO RABATTI): 21 ar, br; ARCHIVIO DoGi (PAOLO SORIANI): 30 bl.

DoGi s.r.l. has made every effort to trace other possible copyright holders. If any omissions or errors have been made, this will be corrected at reprint.